Keynesian Reflections

PARITY
OF THE SEXES

For a complete list of books in the series, see pages 193–194.

PARITY
OF THE SEXES

SYLVIANE AGACINSKI
TRANSLATED BY LISA WALSH

COLUMBIA UNIVERSITY PRESS ◆ NEW YORK

Columbia University Press wishes to express its appreciation for as-sistance given by the government of France through the Ministère de la Culture in the preparation of this translation.

🜲   Columbia University Press
Publishers Since 1893
New York   Chichester, West Sussex

Library of Congress Cataloging-in-Publication Data
Agacinski, Sylviane.
    [Politique des sexes. English]
    Parity of the sexes / Sylviane Agacinski ; translated by Lisa
Walsh.
       p. cm. — (European perspectives)
    Includes index.
    ISBN 0–231–11566–0 (cloth) — ISBN 0–231–11567–9 (pbk.)
    1. Sex role. 2. Sex differences (Psychology). 3. Gender identity.
I. Title. II. Series.
HQ1075 .A43 2001
305.3—dc21   00–047496

CONTENTS

CLARIFICATIONS: PREFACE TO THE ENGLISH-LANGUAGE EDITION

There are times when ideas and events move at the same pace and progress rapidly.

Many of the themes introduced in this book, themes that, in 1998, still only belonged to the domain of theoretical thought, have now made their way into France's legal and political arena. That is the case with the idea of parity, which, within a few years, changed from what many people considered an improbable utopia to a widely shared demand and an institutional reality. Written from a perspective meant to be both philosophical and political, this book will thus continue along its way in a changed context, but one that, I believe, only confirms my positions. Before presenting this edition of *Parity of the Sexes* to the English-language reader, I would like to consider where we stand on a few of the most controversial issues taken up in this work: parity and the principle behind it; the supposed conflict between the value of mixity* and the extension of rights for homosexuals; the articulation of the question concerning the sexes and that of sexualities; the link between medically assisted procreation techniques and the future of sexual difference; and finally, the question of the feminization of certain names and titles in the French language.

PARITY

Candidacy parity between men and women must be respected henceforth by political parties, thanks to a short phrase now added to article 3 of the Constitution. The text does not include the word "parity," but, thanks to the mention of men and women, it lifts the "constitutional bolt" that has prevented legislating in favor of parity. Thus, the masculine monopoly on political power comes to an end and the time for a mixed democracy opens before us. This exemplary speed stems first of all from the obvious anomaly that women's very weak participation in political life until just recently has constituted, but also from the widespread public debate this subject prompted, a debate in which certain chapters of the present work are inscribed. At the end of the debate, the Congress voted, on June 28, 1999, to include in the Constitution that famous little sentence: "The law favors equal access for men and women to electoral mandates and elective offices."

---

*I will be translating the French *mixité* with the English neologism "mixity" in order to maintain the specificity of the term in its implication of the bringing together of two *different* elements. The word *mixité* is most commonly used within the educational context to mean "coeducational," which also adds a connotation of a particularly *sexual* difference. *Tr.*

The application of the principle of parity could then follow rapidly: a law, passed in December 1999, introduced candidacy parity (50/50) for the list system and parity by blocks of six for regional elections or towns with more than 2,500 inhabitants (in order to avoid having women placed at the end of the list); and finally, it encouraged parties to apply parity to legislative elections by means of a financial sanction proportional to their lapses with regard to the equal representation principle.

The democratic invention represented by the principle of parity corresponds to a decisive turning point in French feminism. This turn acknowledges that the abstract equality of individuals *a priori* sexually unspecified does not mitigate the actual exclusion of women from social and political life, that, on the contrary, it conceals it, and that, in order to change existing inequalities stemming from a political history involving only men, it is necessary to consider what a mixed democracy might be.

I must also point out that when writing *Parity of the Sexes*, I did not expect to simply make a contribution to the woman question, and by touching upon that, to the political sphere *stricto sensu*. Most of all, I wanted to show that the question of the duality of the sexes was political from the start, because it involved a duality of perspectives excluding any theoretical overreaching and compromising that scientific neutrality dear to Max Weber. As Thomas Laqueur has shown,[1] scientific discourse on sexual difference has generally shown little concern for factual reality. The simple anatomical or physiological description of male and female characteristics has always been dominated by hierarchical models borrowed from other fields (technical or political, for example). But these models are the product of a perspective so radically androcentric that they have long led specialists to naïvely describe *a single sex* and not two (the other appearing as the mutilated or weaker form of the single male sex). Anthropological research also confirms—notably through the works of Françoise Héritier—that cultures until now have been overwhelmingly androcentric, that a masculine/feminine hierarchy has reigned throughout, and that the male type is generally presented as the single model for humanity. According to this hierarchical structure, woman is neither *the other* nor *different*, but only an incomplete being, inferior or mutilated. The social inequality of the sexes has not been based, as is too often believed, on the recognition of an essential difference; on the contrary, it has simply been inferred from the inferiority of the female type within an essential masculine humankind.

This logic of a single sex, or if you prefer, the identification of humankind with the masculine gender, constitutes the framework for all types of androcentrism. That is why the appeal for unity within humanity has never allowed women to be granted their rightful place. Simone de Beauvoir, with whom it seems to me necessary to part ways on certain points, had already clearly denounced women escaping into the abstraction of "the human being."[2] She knew quite well that this recourse expressed the vain desire to locate oneself "beyond one's sex," as though to finally cease being "in the wrong" in being a woman, whereas a man feels he is "in the right" in being a man.

Nevertheless, it is this flight into the universal abstract that has characterized certain violent antiparity reactions, on the right and the left, expressed in the French press since 1996, directing women to blend into humankind and resist the horrible temptation of "particularism." The rhetoric of republican universalism sounded very beautiful, but it served nevertheless as a screen for maintaining the masculine monopolies on power (political and other) at the same time as it repeated the sleight of hand of all androcentrism, which consists of seeing simultaneously in masculine humanity all of humanity and one of its parts. No one seemed surprised, for example, that the Republic, for so long and so explicitly defined as exclusively male, should wish henceforth, and with such passion, to know nothing of the sex of its citizens, as if there was nothing "particular" about a masculine group, as opposed to its feminine equivalent. Thus, women's ambition to participate equitably in political life could be considered "particularist," but a regime that had always been masculine, by right and in fact, could be considered "universalist." Reference to the rights of women *as such* was denounced as a barbaric return to nature, while the traditional privileges of men *as such* seemed to owe nothing to their sex. With astonishing candor, the guardians of the Republic made an appeal for respecting the difference between neutral culture and sexed nature, as if culture, the law, and politics had, until then, known nothing about the sexes. . . . In reality, the social differentiation between the sexes became intolerable because, for the first time, it was presented as a principle of egalitarian *sharing* between men and women instead of an indication of their inequality, as it had always previously been. Thus, in order for women's place in the polis to finally be recognized, it was necessary to go beyond a sexually neutral idea of democracy and citizenship, and that is the path upon which most feminists and supporters of a mixed society, both men and women, found themselves.

Beyond this *Parity of the Sexes*, it would be necessary to return to consider androcentric logic at greater length as it structures not only the anthropological part of philosophy, but also its metaphysical part. But that will be the subject of a future work. If I began with one credo, it is that *sexual difference is never conceived nor conceivable outside of the sexual controversy (différend)*.

Another revolution has occurred since 1998, and I touch upon the good reasons for it in this book. I am speaking of the creation of the PACS (civil unions). The defenders of the PACS were generally the same people who defended parity to the extent that the desire to rectify the absence of women in social and political life was in perfect harmony with the desire to help homosexuals, male and female, escape the hypocritical invisibility to which the silence of the law and moral disgrace condemned them. The PACS permitted a whole new form of conjugality to be instituted, open to all, and thus as much to mixed couples as to those of the same sex. It constituted some progress toward recognizing and protecting each person's sexual orientation.

However, these two innovations—parity and the PACS—also united a portion of their detractors, in particular those advocating true homosexual marriage, opening the way to adoption and medically assisted procreation rights. They considered the PACS much too watered down an institution, contrasting it to the principle of *equality between couples* (whether homosexual or heterosexual). This new form of egalitarianism, implying a desexualization of individuals, does not easily accommodate any reminders of sexual difference, such as universal duality and the interdependence of the sexes for procreation. Thus, the philosophy of parity is suspected of presenting an obstacle to the rights of homosexuals.

It is true that the possibility of legally giving a child "two parents of the same sex" implies a denial of the mixity of humankind and an erasure of sexual difference. The recognition and value granted to the mixed nature of humanity can only appear very circumspect with regard to the institution of homosexual parenthood, if the latter must at least signify the erasure of the double origin, masculine and feminine, of every child and, consequently, render the sexual identity of the child itself contingent when all is said and done. Thus, the culture of parity seems to want to ensure the equality of the sexes at the expense of "the equality of the sexualities" (sic).

But this conflict exists only if the difference of the sexes and the difference of the "sexualities" are wrongly confused. Sexual orientation relates to the sexualities, whereas sexual difference has always been defined in relation to procreation and filiation. With the PACS, the legalization of homosexuality has no direct connection to the family or marriage because, contrary to what you may read here or there, marriage was not instituted to legalize heterosexuality, but to regulate filiation.

Thus, I renounce nothing in my book that concerns the necessary recognition of the double origin of the child, nor the principle according to which it is not desirable to legally attribute to a child a *parental couple* of the same sex. But I will not confuse this principle with the very different idea that homosexuals ought not to be able to have or to adopt children. In effect, it seems that a distinction must be made between a mixed parental couple, which is one thing, and the individual sexual orientations of those who have or raise children, which is another thing. In other words, one can very easily be parent *and* homosexual, and there are many homosexual parents, but it is not *as homosexual* nor, moreover, *as heterosexual* that one is a father or mother: it is first of all as man or woman, and thus with a second parent of another sex. Furthermore, parenthood seems, for most individuals, to constitute significant proof of finitude and sexual difference.

SEXES AND SEXUALITY

The sexual or amorous bond is not synonymous with the parental bond and sexuality does not have the same meaning as sex. There has always been some gap, or in any case, a potential gap, between the amorous couple and the parental couple. Today, for different reasons than yesterday, the parental relationship, essentially long-lasting, often no longer coincides with the conjugal relationship, and still less often with the now unstable amorous relationship. The distinction between these two types of relationships is assumed not only by "restructured" families but also by homosexuals who have or want to have children without denying the mixity of their origin: "I did not think for a second that I could have a child without a mother," says Marc, who maintains a parental relationship alongside his amorous life; whereas Camille refuses to resort to an anonymous donor, which seems to her a "denial of the father," because she does not intend to maneuver "around the fact that one is born from a father and a mother."[3]

Conversely, the "equality of the couples" theme obscures this distinction between sexuality in the larger sense and the mixity of the origin of children. It requires the construction of the legal couple based upon the amorous couple, and then identifies parents as any couple in general, implying finally that a child must be able to have "two parents, no matter what sex they are." . . . That is something to think about. The problem with this disconcerting formulation, despite the semblance of logic, is that, if we suspend sexual duality, there is no longer any reason why there must be two and only two parents. Why not three fathers, or four mothers? The binary model for the couple is not produced by love or pleasure, but by sexuation, that is, genital differentiation. There are not two parents because they love each other, but because heterogeneity of the race is necessary and sufficient for creating life. On the other hand, sexual practices and amorous ties do not necessarily involve either mixed partners, or even a couple's relationship.

If filiation is generally established in relationship to a couple, it is because it is supported by the representation of the generation process and by an interpretation of the genesis of the embryo. We can make the anthropological hypothesis that alliances respect a bilateral, mixed structure because there must be *at least* two individuals to create life;[4] each of the two plays a *different role* in the origin and development of the embryo. These two *kinds* (*genres*) of individuals have been named *sexes*, genetically complementary, together forming the entire humankind. Thus—and speaking in a deliberately *crude* fashion here—the sexual condition of humanity, made up of males and females, like all higher animals, has no other basic definition than the one referring back to procreation, regardless of the many social forms this dichotomy can give rise to. There can be infinite variety in the social sense of this dichotomy, but no obliterating its necessity in the order of *generation*.

That is why the universal model for the parental couple is the *mixed* couple, and not, as is sometimes very oddly claimed, the *heterosexual* couple. This is not at all the same thing. Filiation is not concerned with "sexualities," but it has never ignored the two sexes, for which the legal parental couple is no doubt an institutional representation. Even in exceptional cases, like that of marriage between women, as among the Nuer of Africa, this union is not linked to homosexuality and does not contradict the schema of the mixed parental couple. What sort of configuration is this? A reputedly sterile woman can marry one or many women who will give her children for whom she will then be the "father." We can see that this marriage is only possible because the sterile woman has been made masculine by the institution. Thus, this is a matter of the fiction of a mixed marriage and not the institutionalization of a two-woman couple (parallel to which the natural mixed origin survives, since a man must be called upon to fulfill the male generative function). Of course, we may conclude from this, along with Françoise Héritier, that "*it is not sex, but fertility, that determines the real difference between the masculine and the feminine.*"[5] But we could also say that, in the end, there is no definition of sex other than the one that relies upon difference as the principle of generation, and this is where the only *point of departure* for masculine and feminine is located.

That is why sexual difference cannot be deconstructed by opposing different models of "sexualities" (for example, "hetero" and "homo"), which finally have nothing to do with the difference of the sexes. It is legitimate to demand freedom of sexualities or to call into question the model of the heterosexual couple (even though heterosexuality is not always a matter of a couple, or a single couple, model). But there is no reason to throw the baby, sexual difference, out with the bath water, heterocentrism and homophobia.

Femininism and Sexualities

The only event actually requiring the duality of the sexes is birth. This in no way prejudges a certain vagueness about the "genders"—in a psychological or cultural sense, noticeable, moreover, even among heterosexuals. In this sense, it is not necessary to postulate a simple sexual identity for each person. Still less to try at any cost to replace basic sexual identity (that which differentiates men and women) with an identity of sexuality that opposes heterosexuals to homosexuals.

This substitution would be all the more illogical as neither heterosexuality nor homosexuality—if we want to signify by these words a fixed structure of desire—can have meaning without reference to sexual difference and the discrimination desire then makes. Moreover, the general category of "homosexual couples," if it tends to suspend the man/woman distinction, finally echoes old homophobic discourse, which has always contested the sexual identity of homosexuals, as if, by choice, they were inevitably betraying their sex, as if gays could not be men and lesbians could not be women. It is just as strange to construct a single category for gay and lesbian sexuality, as if, outside of heterosexuality, itself wrongly unified, there were no more than one possible sexuality. My hypothesis, which remains to be verified, is that, on the contrary, the deepest difference is still the one distinguishing men and women with their diverse sexualities, whether heterosexuals or homosexuals. Certainly, there are not more similarities between male and female homosexualities than there are between the sexes.

By the same token, we can ask ourselves what basis there is, from a theoretical or political perspective, for gays and lesbians to be assembled in a single camp, outside of the necessary struggle against homophobia. This union is nearly as problematic as the one that consists of uniting the struggles of homosexuals (men and women) and feminists into one, under the pretext that they are both victims of discrimination. Of course, nothing stands in the way, quite the contrary, of fighting on many fronts at the same time, and campaigning for the recognition of minorities' rights. But—and this is one of the main themes of this book—it is an intellectual and political mistake to liken women to a minority. Feminism always risks being trapped by a neutralization of sexual difference, thus giving free rein to androcentrism, omnipresent and active everywhere.

It is evident, on the contrary, that androcentrism ran through all the "liberation movements" (workers, communists, leftists, etc.) leading to the rebirth of feminism after 1968. It had become clear that no political or economic revolution would bring to an end the ancestral, many-faceted, sexual hierarchy.

It is possible that androcentrism still runs through the homosexual movement today and that the "deconstruction" of the sexes advocated by "queer" culture, including by women, only contributes, once again, to obscuring their existence and their rights.

In France, the theoretical movement that works to deny or "deconstruct" sexual difference (even though it is the sexual hierarchy that needs to be criticized), has for some time laid the blame on psychoanalysis, denounced as a bastion of a conservative "symbolic order," inasmuch as it has not eliminated the sexual difference. I am well aware that reputations shape reactions, but neither Freud nor Lacan invented sexual duality. They explored the psychological figures or configurations that this duality was able to produce, notably regarding the structure of desire, and its bisexual, heterosexual, and homosexual forms. Psychoanalysis has even rather helped to free sexuality from genitalia, and thus from the "solid base" of sexual generation, since it is only after Freud that it is possible to speak of sexuality and even more, *sexualities*, in the plural, in the present sense of equally legitimate libidinal choices.

Thus, Freud opened an immense field to the understanding of desire, or rather, desires. From the perspective in question here, however, I believe that the foundations and effects of Freudian thought have not been examined thoroughly enough. We are not sufficiently astonished that psychoanalysis was able to give sexual difference a psychological status that paid so little attention to the dissymmetry in the order of fertility.

Without being able to develop this point at length, I will say that, by constructing a theory of sexuality centered on the libido, or in other words, on love, its subject and its object, Freud was not able to avoid developing an androcentric order, despite (or because of?) the newness of his field. He designated a male anatomical attribute as the locus of sex, inescapably assigning to female anatomy an absence or a mystery.

Of course, psychoanalysis became tied up with the psychological aspect of sexuality. But it did not do that without articulating in an original way the physical facts, in this case anatomical, especially with regard to sexual difference. As I stress in one chapter of this book, it is easy to show, and this task has not been neglected, that it is through a *boy's view* that Freud responded to the infantile question of sexual difference. In passing, the case of the little girl is immediately assimilated to that of the boy in such a way that she can only intensely envy the precious male attribute and that her femininity is definitively inscribed into a *logic of lack* and castration that, at best, the child will come to compensate for. Once programmed, this androcentric logic will indeed mark the whole history of female sexuality to the point of deriving from it the child's desire for castration and the all too famous "penis envy" attributed to girls.

A less historicist perspective, searching less in childhood for the genesis of desire, less dependent, also on the visible order, would allow further investigation into the male and female positions in genital sexual life. Perhaps we would then discover a dissymmetry so profound that it would finally prohibit thinking of one sex beginning from the other. Because we must ask ourselves—and I believe that this is the book's main intuition—*if men and women speak of the same thing when they speak of sex or the sexes.* If this suspicion could be verified, that would mean that there is no shared measure between the masculine and the feminine and that what is called sexual difference is to be considered an irreducible ontological duality, impossible to reconcile or synthesize.

From an empirical perspective, we can note, for example, that for women, a physical contiguity exists between all sexual events, from the sexual act itself to the various phases of childbirth (if it occurs). That is undoubtedly why women have often rejected, abandoned, or killed children born out of violence or rape. Medea takes revenge on Jason through her children. Conversely, the man is confronted with fertility and gestation as an event external to his body and not directly continuous with him. Such dissymmetry implies that the man is in a discontinuous relationship with fertility and in a necessarily ambivalent relationship to the power of women. Moreover, what does male desire have to do with children? Freud does not say much about this, except, in a general way, linking it to the desire for eternity. But, if the desire to engender children exists in the man, what about his heteronomy with regard to the process and the place—female—of childbirth? Isn't this heteronomy capable of producing some psychological effects, no less important that those produced by the all too famous anatomical difference?

The consequences of the dissymmetry just mentioned have been examined to a greater extent—and better—by anthropology than by psychoanalysis. Anthropologists, in particular women anthropologists, have not failed to note that the ancestral incertitude that strikes at the paternal origin of a child, whereas the maternal origin is clear, constitutes an alienation of masculine fertility. This cannot help but shed light on why men wish to appropriate their offspring by appropriating one or several women. It also explains why they have tried to bestow upon themselves the true power to engender and have, almost everywhere, theorized about the preeminent role, even the exclusive role, of the father in the transmission of life (generally through the role of the sperm). But this primacy of the paternal role cannot completely do away with the dissymmetry or the natural inequality of maternal and paternal positions in childbirth: maternity is, first of all, a state, while paternity is always a title. This dissymmetry is prior to the order of legal kinship, which seems, rather, a result of the need to institutionalize a usually uncertain paternity. Saint Augustine already understood all this: "Marriage was instituted, in order that, thanks to the chastity of women, sons would be known by their fathers and fathers by their sons."[6] Thus, paternity is never the masculine equivalent of maternity, no more than maternity is the feminine equivalent of paternity. Sexual difference designates nothing other that this *absence of equivalence*, even if other differences also exist on many levels of sexual life. It prevents us from considering man and woman to be interchangeable.

Thus, of course, the heirs of Platonism can continue to see in sexual difference and generation only the irrational, animal part of the human, as if this part ought to remain foreign to the higher preoccupations of a philosophic or political order. But this metaphysical obscuring of sexual difference always derives from the philosophical contempt reserved for generation and descent. A philosophy of finitude, on the other hand, must rethink generation and consider how, for humanity, it is the source of ethics and constitutes a proof of time and transcendence.

Finally, the primary dissymmetry between the sexes could shed light on the current data concerning a possible technical appropriation of procreation, and technology overtaking the interdependence of the sexes. Indeed, this dissymmetry reminds us of something very interesting: that the relationship of the father to fertility has always been, basically, comparable—and compared—to that of an artisan to his work, and that, with regard to gestation and birth, he has always had the distant relationship of a spectator viewing a process that remains external to him.

PROCREATION TECHNOLOGY AND THE FUTURE OF SEXUAL DIFFERENCE

Intoxicated by the modern ideal of an all-powerful science and technology, our epoch dreams of being able to control reproduction from without.

A completely external process of fertilization and gestation is now conceivable, if not foreseeable. The mastery of an entirely disembodied reproduction process would allow us to imagine a decline or an end to sexual differentiation—even if cloning alone, practiced with the help of an artificial uterus, would abolish the interdependence of the sexes, indeed even allow for just one of them to survive. What a lovely prospective war between the sexes for science fiction lovers! This takes place, we should note, at the very moment when women in modern societies have acquired control over their bodies, fertility, and lineage. A radical reversal of the patriarchal order. Technical disembodiment of childbirth calls back into question a recently won female power. Nevertheless, the idea of entirely technologically controlled procreation, which would then enter into the order of artisanal or industrial production, is hardly disquieting to everyone. On the contrary, it satisfies those who see in it a new freedom and the possibility of a new right: "the right to do without one's body for procreation."[7] It offers a solution especially to individuals who, for whatever reason (sterility or homosexuality), cannot have children through natural bodily means.

Let us take this opportunity to remind those made uneasy by nature, who think they must reject the "natural" and the "biological" in one gesture, that these two ideas are neither synonymous nor equivalent. There is only an autonomous biological order since the development of a techno-biological sphere focused on *depersonalized* cells and living materials. It is only with the existence of this sphere that biology makes the law, in a wholly novel fashion. Formerly, we spoke of natural children, but we did not know about this biological "kinship" whose traces we are now going to pursue even into the grave.

Be that as it may, because of the dissymmetry we spoke of earlier, there would not be anything very new, from the male perspective, in the technological externalization of procreation, since, in fact, the man (as father) had always procreated outside of his own body, and since paternity has always basically been of a legal order for him. Thus, in some way, he has always had the "right to do without his body to procreate."[8]

Thus arises the question of knowing if, by claiming to free humanity from bodily constraints, biotechnologies are not obeying a new androcentric programming, even if remedies for female sterility are sometimes found there. Because, by allowing the two sexes to be technologically emancipated from their interdependence and physical constraints, they also make more widespread a *masculine model of procreation*, that is, one of reproduction *outside the body*. The old male/female controversy over control of descendancy may take the new form of a rivalry between embodied procreation and technical procreation.

Nevertheless, until the present, human sociability has been woven from interdependence and alliance between sexes and generations. The link of mortals to their ancestors and their descendants, as strong as it is ambivalent, generally wards off individual egocentric fantasies of omnipotence. It is not clear that that must change, given the tenacious attraction the two sexes continue to exercise over each other. But, if it were to go otherwise, if, as individuals, we all had to be related to our children like manufactured products, and to our parents like sponsors, humanity would experience the most profound transformation in its history, with incalculable consequences. Undoubtedly we could say: Why not? But let us not pretend to believe that sexual difference has no other significance or meaning than that of hampering "the equality of couples." We can combat homophobia and heterocentrism without imagining we must abolish sexual difference at the same time. In fact, it is not the diversity of sexualities that calls into question our sexual condition, *it is the conjunction of fanatical individualism and biotechnological temptations.*

Finally, we must remember that sexual duality does not belong to a single, limited anthropological field. It does not only concern men and women, and their psychology and anatomy; it also speaks to us about animals and gods, mythology and theology, biology and metaphysics (and it would be necessary to write these all in the plural).

The French Language and the Feminine

I will close this preface in the form of clarifications by confessing to an inexcusable absence in this *Parity of the Sexes*, an issue that has also given rise to many debates: the place of the feminine in the language.

In this regard, I regret not having recognized sooner the justness of the positions of Benoîte Groult, a pioneer in the subject[9] who has understood for a very long time how a certain effacement of the feminine, in French (in the sense of effacing oneself before another, letting the other be first), has reflected and reinforced the traditional reticence of women, their scarcity in public and political spheres, as in all places of power. Thus, the current promotion of women in our societies has sometimes brought with it new uses for the feminine, sometimes the feminization of masculine nouns.

The Academie française has tried for some time to resist the feminization of titles and offices by hiding behind grammatical logic, as if it fell from the sky, without understanding that the alleged neutrality of the masculine, which our Academicians insist upon calling the *non marqué*, or unmarked, gender, was in fact the linguistic mark of an old social order and the symbolic relic of androcentrism in our culture and our language.

It is all too clear that the traditional absence of women in the public space (the sphere of nondomestic economic activities, the political and cultural milieu, etc.) was accompanied by an absence of feminine forms in the French vocabulary. The masculine was necessarily dominant in the language, all the more so because it was also supposed to signify the two sexes (for example, in the plural: *les habitants*), to designate a category deliberately "unmarked" (*l'usager, le lecteur*) or again, because of the so-called epicene nouns, which have only one gender no matter what the sex of the individuals in question: "assassin," "witness," "counterfeiter," and "monster" remain masculine in French, but so do "author" and "printer." A few epicenes are feminine, like "beast" and "victim," and again, the famous "sentinel," unfailingly cited by those out to prove that epicenes are not sexist. But you do not need witchcraft to show that most of the so-called masculine epicenes are, in fact, the names of occupations formerly practiced exclusively by men. Grevisse[10] does not fail to emphasize this when giving a list of masculine epicenes that includes, for example, "architect," "author," "minister," "painter," "plumber," "pilot," and "fashion designer." The last noun is particularly symptomatic of this hierarchy of genders that reflects the social sexual hierarchy: the dressmaker (*la couturière*) is inevitably small, the fashion designer (*le grand couturier*) inevitably great. Today, certain conservative grammarians pretend to confuse the names of occupations with the epicenes, or again, with the alleged neutrality of the masculine, as if French did not normally match gender with a person's sex. The oldest usage clearly denies this thesis as soon as activities are actually practiced by women. In the 1930s, a less nervous time than today, the Immortals did not hesitate to create feminine forms for "aviator," "lawyer," "voter," and "candidate" (even though France at that time still scoffed at the suffragettes). In fact, most of the time, French matches the grammatical gender with the sex: *un paysan, une paysanne, un danseur, une danseuse*. Thus, usage very logically imposes the progressive feminization of the names of positions, titles, and occupations when they refer to women and when the structure of the language is not harmed by it. It is completely natural for us to say *une dentiste* or *une ministre*.

Nevertheless, this legitimate tendency runs up against the absence of the feminine, which it must then construct, or again, the existence of an anachronistic feminine. Indeed, French has made wide use of a feminine that I would call "matrimonial," since it serves to name women based exclusively on their role as spouse. As with so many other feminine nouns, for a long time, *pharmacienne* designated the wife of a pharmacist, as the *ambassadrice* was the spouse of the ambassador, the *mairesse* the wife of the mayor, not to mention the *étudiante*, which at one time signified the lover of a student (*étudiant*)![11] These examples speak for themselves and offer sufficient reason to break with a usage according to which women have no other status—nor other name—than that of their spouse or lover. The uncalled-for survival of the matrimonial feminine leaves women the titles they owe to their husbands, whereas it is important to grant them those they themselves deserve. In defending these throwbacks, Maurice Druon shows that he does not understand the new feminine usage, denounced as "counter to grammatical sense."[12] But shouldn't the former permanent Secretary consider what runs counter to *historical* sense as well as the anachronism into which he himself falls?

French has never been sparing with the feminine for domestic labors or manual professions, and the Académie willingly recognizes that "usage has long been established for feminine forms with regard to trades, like baker, delicatessen or grocery shop keeper."

Nevertheless, this gender seems ill-suited to noble occupations or higher positions. One discriminating intelligence has even dared to write that the "sexualization" of public titles would deprive women of their true conquest, "authority, responsibility, power," since "*This is said grammatically in the masculine.*"[13] Whoa! I am not sure that grammar deserves to be conscripted into so questionable a cause. It seems futile to get bogged down in sexist quibbling that finally runs counter to the spirit of a language capable of playing with all the possibilities: agreement of gender and sex, occasional departures, but also the disturbing mix of masculine and feminine, as when Flaubert wrote in such a lovely way to Georges Sand "*chère bon maître*," "dear" (feminine) "good master" (masculine).

No one wants to violate linguistic structures or systematically add the feminine to the masculine where the plural, for example, can signify both genders to good advantage. It is more economical to address the reader (*au lecteur*, masculine) than to use "*au lecteur et à la lectrice*," or to speak of the inhabitants of a city (*habitants*, masculine) rather than "des habitants et des habitantes"—although this principle of economy, which the grammars set forth in saying that "the masculine prevails over the feminine," remains the expression of a kind of grammatical struggle between the genders, in which the masculine continues to "prevail"! Be that as it may, such economy does not apply when it comes to naming the woman pharmacist, representative, secretary (even Secretary of State), police officer, lawyer, historian, or philosopher (*la pharmacienne, la députée, la secretaire*, etc.) In the linguistic and symbolic fields, as in others, using the two genders, or mixed forms (when changing the determiner is enough) will henceforth, without a doubt, accompany the presence and visibility of women in public life. And so much the better if this or that word survives as evidence of the ever possible conflict between sex and gender, like "mannequin," "model" (both masculine), "star," or "weakling" (both feminine), with their ambiguous effects.

Thus, this book's most constant claim is that the duality of the sexes—whether viewed as a universal existential condition or as a social differentiation, with its specific cultural and historic forms—will not allow itself to be reduced or passed over, but only, and no doubt indefinitely, to be *practiced*. The thinking about this duality, as with the relationships between the sexes, will thus endlessly transform through time.

PREFACE

Never before had I so wanted to write a book. I began working without premeditation, as if under the effect of a personal necessity, abandoning the work in progress.

External circumstances, however, also figured into the equation. In June 1996, women politicians, transcending their usual divisions, issued a manifesto for parity calling for voluntary measures to establish effective equality between men and women in instances of decision making. Effective equality also meant quantitative balance, because in France only 5.5 percent of the National Assembly and 5.6 percent of the Senate were then women. The debate on parity, which quickly took on significance in the public arena, awakened me from a long sleep. At the time I was a bit weary of the "woman question" and feminist struggles, which, it seemed to me, had in large part attained their goals, at least in our country. Looking in my personal library, then, for a work on the history of feminism—in light of these circumstances—I realized that most of the books devoted to the "woman question" were very high up, on shelves almost out of reach. The thick layer of dust covering them suddenly made me conscious of the layer of indifference between this question and myself that had accumulated over the past fifteen years.

Why, then, this sudden mobilization? Because, if parity was bringing together majority opinion, it was also deeply dividing women themselves. As we know, it was feminists who launched the fiercest objections to parity, even if these objections did find eager allies among the conservatives of the right—and the left.

The polemic that developed demonstrated that the ideal of parity, with this absolutely novel demand on the part of women to *share* political power with men, was literally exploding the vague consensus that seemed to reign in France as to the equality of the sexes and the validity of feminist struggles in general.

As for me, I was convinced by the originality and audacity of the demand of parity already advanced by several woman pioneers.

Parity seemed all the more interesting to me for the way it somehow combined two ideas into one: it simultaneously constituted a new approach to *sexual difference** by giving it a political meaning and a new approach to *democracy* by entrusting it with the realization of the equality of the sexes, not in a *better* way, but *otherwise*.

This idea was truly worthy of public debate, and it is to contribute to that debate, as much as to clarify my own positions, that I immediately began to reconsider the woman question, or at least the question of "mixity." Because man is double and not single, divided and not *one*, and it is this division that must be contemplated.

**La différence des sexes* is translated as "sexual difference" rather than "the difference of the sexes" for ease of reading, since Agacinski seems to use *la différence des sexes* and *la différence sexuelle* in the same sense. *Tr.*

It is not by chance that this bone of contention, parity, was the outcome of a concerted action among women politicians, since the conviction that democracy still had progress to make with regard to the equality of men and women—and that the matter had decidedly been poorly undertaken—was born at the heart of political life. This explains the radical exigency of the demand for parity, but it is not by chance, because until this point feminism had strictly maintained a separation between its own specific claims and political struggles.

Certainly, the emancipation of women was obviously a political struggle, but its stakes were, for the most part, judicial or social. On the other hand, elsewhere the work of reflection upon sexual difference was very profitably pursued in the realms of philosophy, the social sciences, and literature. But no one seemed to be interested in power or political institutions.

From the end of World War II until the nineties, women have maintained a distance from power or direct political stakes, or else have not believed in the necessity of a separate feminist course of action. This was the case of leftist women who, according to Marxist or socialist analyses, trusted revolutionary struggles to put an end to all forms of alienation. Even Simone de Beauvoir had this point of view. Likewise, post-1968 feminism ignored political power as such, sometimes for these same reasons but more often because it wanted to put up a radical resistance to the political (and masculine) order already in place. This was the period when certain factions of the MLF,* far from caring about the just repre-

---

*MLF is an acronym designating *Mouvement de Libération des Femmes* (Movement for the Liberation of Women). The French press coined the term in 1970 to collectively name "radical" feminist groups. MLF has come to signify the women's rights movement as a whole in France. *Tr.*

sentation of women in the *Assemblées*, affirmed that women were "not representable."

Thus, women's indifference with regard to political power was the effect of dual junctures: a global, political climate in which power was contested and democracy scorned, and a historical, moral, and cultural situation that justified other priorities for women, such as the struggle for access to contraception and abortion. Assuredly, the achievement of these freedoms was more urgent.

The collapse of the Berlin wall, the erosion of the ideology of class struggle and the extinction of the State, the awakening of the philosophy of human rights after the totalitarian nightmares: all this contributed to the rehabilitation of democracy and to the renewed reflection upon its principles and operation. It is within this context that women's new interest in politics and the innovative claims often accompanying it must be situated.

But if the objective of parity comes to unmask feminism's latent contradictions, it is because parity implements a politicization of sexual difference. While the first feminism, an offshoot of Simone de Beauvoir's analyses in *The Second Sex*, relied principally on the equalization of rights and conditions, and demanded the right to *indifference* with regard to the sexual identity of individuals, parity requires the *rethinking* of this difference. Women who still defend the "indifferentialist" position are relatively isolated. Most women who wanted to advance the cause of women took sexual difference into account, and beyond these political divisions they united— today, behind the necessity of parity, as yesterday, behind that of the legalization of abortion.[1]

Expressing the need for the representative assemblies to be effectively mixed rather than remain practically masculine monopolies, parity breaks with the universalist doctrine of the neutrality or the indifference of the sexes. Parity considers that the people and its representatives are sexed[2] individuals, masculine and feminine, who, as such, should be equally in charge of the public domain.

But let's not get ahead of ourselves. We will try to shed some light on this question in the pages that follow.

Let's just say that the will to share power between men and women can only be legitimate if we admit that sex is neither a social nor a cultural *trait*, nor an ethnic one, that it is not the common characteristic of some "community"—like a language, a religion, or a territory—but, rather, that it is a *universal*, differential trait. That is, humankind* does not exist outside this double form, masculine and feminine.

In order to consider what may be a politics of the sexes, and today, a politics of women, I should first pause at this very difficult question, a question that can have no definitive answer: What is this sexual difference that founds a difference of kind or gender, and ensures that in no culture are masculine and feminine ever confused, any more than are men and women?

As is to be expected, difference will not reveal all its secrets, because, if it is truly imposed by nature, inductive of the law of a procreation always divided between a masculine *and* feminine origin, it is societies and civilizations that give difference a meaning. Thus, there is no truth to the difference of the sexes; rather, there is an endless ef-

---

*Here, Agacinski uses the French *genre humain*, which has been translated as "humankind," as opposed to *race humaine* (human race) or *espèce humaine* (human species). It should be noted that the French *genre*, aside from its traditional meaning as "kind," has come to take on the somewhat anglicized meaning of "gender." Agacinski will later make use of the double signification of "genre." *Tr.*

fort on the part of humanity to give it meaning, to interpret it, to cultivate it. If we are conscious of this, the question also becomes political: What meaning, today, do we wish to recognize or lend to the mixity of humanity?

We cannot merely be neutral observers of any and all interpretations. We have a vested interest in theories of difference, as well as the respective places of men and women in a culture—particularly our own. Thus we must radically challenge the hierarchy of the sexes and the valorization of masculine models. But we must also accept sexual difference, recognize therein the origin of human diversity, and found upon it the demand for new ways of sharing power.

This is why I wanted to write a book that would be both a philosophical reflection in its argument and a political stand in the choices it considers. I write to show that it is perhaps unnecessary to wish, at any price, ignorance or denial of the fact that man is divided. The diversity, the dissymmetry, and even the conflict that result from this division are fortunate and not an affliction, as much for men as for peoples and communities. Beyond the possible disagreements between the sexes, it is important that they agree, at least, on this fundamental and perhaps misunderstood value: the universal mixity of humanity that should, in a more general way, initiate each sex into the recognition of the other.

Isn't the other sex, for each, the closest face of the *stranger*? Thus it is crucial, politically, to know how sexual difference is recognized or, on the contrary, denied. Because the way we think the *other* sex determines the way we think the *other* in general.

TRANSLATOR'S ACKNOWLEDGMENTS

I would like to thank Jody Gladding for her time and energy in revising the first version of the translation.

My very deepest appreciation to Jaaron Sanderson, whose painstaking work on the final revisions of the translation is in large part responsible for an authentic and readable rendering of the French text.

PARITY
OF THE SEXES

PART IV

STRATEGIES

Differences

In order that there might be a world, it is, indeed, necessary to pass from the one to the two, and "two" is the path which opens onto the multiple, the thousands, the millions. Two is, so to speak, the one of the multiple, the opening, birth.

—Jean-Christophe Bailly[1]

ℿAℿ DⅰVⅰDED

One is born a girl or boy, one becomes woman or man.

The human species is divided in two, and, like most other species, in two only. This division, which includes all human beings without exception, is thus a dichotomy. In other words, every individual who is not man is woman. There is no third possibility.

The apparent simplicity of this duality, as we know, conceals complications, in so far as nature seems to have hesitated at times. But it is not so much androgyny that poses a question—it is much the exception—as sexual identity in general. Far from depending solely on an anatomical program, sexual identity concerns conscious and unconscious choices and engages social models. The way in which each person perceives his own identity, or experiences his desires, cannot be described by simple figures or alternatives.* The division of the

---

*To avoid repetition of "his or her," I have translated possessive pronouns in the masculine, although in French the gender of the possessor is ambiguous. I have

species allows itself to be recognized in each individual, and each of us, man or woman, is also, fortunately, a bit mixed. To say that man** is divided, then, is not simply to speak of the division of the human kind, but also of each "individual," who, though his name does not indicate it, is himself divided. The consciousness of this division of humankind has the effect that each person knows, or should know, that he himself is, for the other sex, the *other*.

Difference traverses every individual of both sexes, affecting each with a certain bisexuality. The recognition of this duality, which was largely Freud's doing, has no effect on the dual structure itself. It only creates, in each subject, the infinite possibility of play that might engage masculine and feminine, consciously or unconsciously—starting with the simple coexistence of opposites and moving through alternation (now one/then the other), contradiction (either/or), or any number of other arrangements.

Even though the division of the sexes is my object here, I am not forgetting that each person is, above all a singularity, and thus that no one trait, sexual or otherwise, could determine him as a member of a collection of identical individuals. But, having said this, the absolute singularity of each existence does not rid us of the question of gender.

The fact that there is no necessary causal relation between biological and psychological identity, between anatomical sex and sexual, social *gender*, does not in any way exclude the principle of dif-

------

chosen the masculine rather than the feminine as it corresponds more closely to the author's argument. *Tr.*

**The author uses the masculine collective, "man," to refer to the universal human. I have chosen to keep the author's usage as her argument is in large part constructed as a response to a masculine universal exclusive of mixity. *Tr.*

ference. Nor can biological difference be made relative by invoking, for example, the desire on the part of certain individuals to change their sex and the current attempts to achieve this through surgeries. One can take the physical attributes of an individual's sex away and give him those of the other. Nor does the deliberate inversion of traditional models of masculine and feminine behavior—the father playing the role of the mother, or vice versa—subvert the principle of duality in models of cultural forms. This inversion only shows that these models are partly conventional and that they, too, allow for play. These models can certainly be transformed, but they attest to a certain distinction that culture cannot seem to do without.

These supposed subversions only confirm the inevitability of division. He—or she—who wishes to "change sex," that is, to have a surgeon create a sex organ in conformity with his "*true* gender" in order to replace the one he was endowed with at birth, transposes the physical sexual division at the most intimate level of the soul. He feels the imperious and inborn nature of his profound sexual identity: his "soul," he says, is a woman's soul in a man's body—or vice versa. He seems to consider souls more imperatively sexed than bodies. But, through their request or demand for physical transformation, transsexuals reveal, often with much pathos, their need for a sexual definition as much psychic* as it is anatomical or social. They need to take on all the real or symbolic attributes of the *gender* they want to have . . . or rather, *to be*, so much that they seem to be suf-

---

Psychique in French, translated quite traditionally here as "psychic," refers to that which pertains to the psyche and, unlike its English cognate, has no paranormal connotations. *Tr.*

fer from the necessity of a unique sexual identity.[2] Thus, in its own way, transsexualism reinforces the potency of the sexual dichotomy, even when a woman claims to be a man "for lack of feeling like a woman," all the while regretting that there is no third term.[3] Transsexualism has nothing to do with "a transvestite's regime" characteristic of our time.[4] The transsexual is not satisfied with cross-dressing alone, he believes too much in nature and the tyrannical ties that bind sex and gender. For him, clothes are not a prosthesis any more than the organ he believes he may have grafted on; if he believed in simulacra, he would not need a surgeon.

Quite to the contrary, we feel that sexual identity must be played out again and again, that one must always "add more" to become what one "is." A woman who puts on high heels and lipstick is perfectly conscious that *she disguises herself as a woman*. But then again, if you can't judge a book by its cover, can you judge a man or a woman by his or hers? This notion has become commonplace since we seem to have admitted that nature no longer exists. We both believed and defended, most often with good reason, the notion that nature, responsible for all inequalities and injustices, must be silenced because it had previously had too much of a voice. No more nature, no more sexes: difference became a question of history, culture, and clothes.

It is time to open our eyes again: just because sexual difference is always represented, acted out, symbolized, does not mean it is nothing, or owes nothing, to nature. A woman is always somewhat "disguised" as a woman (less and less today perhaps), but she has great difficulty disguising herself as a man, and vice versa. "You see [Colette has someone say to Amalia], when a woman remains a woman, she is a complete human being. She lacks nothing, even in her 'girlfriend's' opinion. But if she ever gets it into her head to try to be a man, then she's grotesque."[5]

Nevertheless, transvestites do not lack charm, but this charm lies in the ambiguity that jumps out at us. They are always troubling or disturbing because they show two sexual identities at once. They create a dizzying gaze that cannot definitively rest upon one identity or the other. But, here too, the duality being played with is thereby confirmed.

There is as much naïveté in wanting to return the sexes to their pure nature as in denouncing their difference as simply an effect of arbitrary historical construction. Sexual difference is very real, it is a matter of natural, physical givens. To put it simply, as completely natural it is *meaningless*. Only when cultivated does it have meaning. Thus, if it's already been interpreted, it's already been disguised.

Culture, we might say, with its clothes and prostheses, is the art of cultivating natural differences. This is why sexual difference is more effectively treated by artists than by scientists or philosophers, who always believe that the truth can be revealed.

But man is naturally a disguised animal. He does not exist without clothing or habits, which are ways of making *folds* in nature. Nature, therefore, must have an aptitude for folding, a certain suppleness, a certain *plasticity*.* (Thus the question of sexual difference always corresponds with questions of fashion. Inversely, the arts of fashion are essentially occupied with sexual difference.)

Indeed, where do the tastes for plastic differentiation—accentuating traits and playing with forms—come from if they are not al-

---

*The expression "*les arts plastiques*," more widely used in French than its English counterpart, the plastic arts, refers to arts whose goal is the elaboration of forms such as sculpture, architecture, drawing, and even choreography. Hence Agacinski's use of "*plasticité*" (plasticity) and "*plastique*" (plastic) should be understood in this context of malleable forms. *Tr.*

ready in this natural variation of the species that produces masculine and feminine bodies? The natural duality of the plastic human is like an originary theme from which are derived the formal variations of art.

It is not certain that sexual dualism can be escaped, regardless of the diversity of variations in which it might appear. This is one of the lessons of Françoise Héritier's book *Masculin/Féminin: La Pensée de la différence.*[6] Indeed, this anthropologist demonstrates that sexual difference, as natural biological given, furnishes a general, differential structure that all cultures will translate, each in its own way. Nature creates difference, and the reading of this difference produces the universal, symbolic alphabet of the masculine/feminine couple with which each culture "makes sentences." In other words, each society invents cultural constructions and social organizations that combine the masculine and the feminine in different ways. I can only echo Héritier on this point: beginning from its biological "anchoring," the masculine/feminine difference universally constitutes a model that structures societies, although the values and contents given to this difference vary according to the culture.

However, we must also admit that until now sexual difference, both always and everywhere, has taken on the meaning of a *hierarchy*. The masculine is always proclaimed to be superior to the feminine, no matter how these categories are applied. This is what Héritier calls "the differential valence of the sexes." Not only does sexual difference play a structuring role throughout but, in addition, the two sexes are never given equal value. The masculine is always said to be superior to the feminine.

Confirmations of this hierarchy appear in the most unexpected places. For example, in the nineteenth century, taking a position once again in the old artistic debate over line and color, a theoretician might write: "Line is the masculine sex of art; color is the feminine. . . . Line must maintain its preponderance over color."[7] When color comes to be recognized as the essential component of painting, Matisse will say that color is the virile element of painting, line being the feminine part. . . .

The existence of this hierarchy is manifest in all *androcentric* systems, that is, those placing men at the center, or at the summit, of hierarchies. Androcentrism can just as easily characterize a social organization as a system of representations or concepts. It can constitute, as we shall see, a way of effacing the duality of the sexes and assimilating it into a masculine "universality."

However, if we cannot abolish sexual difference and its structuring role through, most notably, systems of kinship, and if the Western tradition is, to a large extent, marked by androcentrism, we can question the possibilities for transforming these ancient hierarchies and for giving other values to sexual difference and other roles to men and women. This is a question posed by historian Arlette Farge, who hopes that history might allow for "the deciphering of historical moments in which the power relations between the sexes are examined and constituted in a different way than before."[8]

The possibility of transforming relations between the sexes exists, we know, but it is necessarily *philosophical and political*. Philosophical, if we believe that philosophy can and should contribute to modifying our way of thinking. Political, if we believe that political forces and actions can and should transform the organization of societies, notably, relations between the sexes. To philosophy and politics let us add the arts, which harbor a power to interpret and thus to transform the real. We know more about man and woman through mythology, literature, poetry, painting, theater, opera, film, and dance than through any natural science.

To the extent that they study facts, including physical facts, and to the extent that they claim to describe the real and produce concepts capable of making the real intelligible, the social sciences sometimes forget that human reality is most immediately a matter of art—that is to say, a matter of a cultivated nature, one susceptible to mutations. The knowledge of what is, as it is, always contains a certain risk of producing conservative effects if we consider the resistance of facts or the stability of a structure as the consequence of an absolute and immutable necessity.

Psychoanalysis and anthropology have thus conceptualized androcentrism because this construction does, in effect, emerge from both unconscious formations and structures of kinship. Jacques Lacan calmly relies on Lévi-Strauss when he says that "the symbolic order is androcentric in its initial functioning. *It is a fact.*"[9] Lacan knows very well that this "fact," associated with the place of women in alliance systems between lineages, has gone through all sorts of modifications throughout history, but he argues, nonetheless, that androcentrism remains "fundamental," and that it permits "an understanding of the dissymmetrical position of woman in amorous relations."

Now, even if to think about mixity is to think about difference and the dissymmetries it implies, this does not necessarily entail considering androcentrism a fundamental given that escapes history and the transformations it can bring about. Today's dissymmetries are not yesterday's: just think about women's control of their own fertility. Without a doubt, this new power will have consequences for the symbolic order and effects on the unconscious that are still immeasurable today.

Androcentrism, expressed in Lacan by "the primacy of the phallus" in the symbolic order, was already present in Freud with the idea that there is only one libido and that, as an activity of the drives, it is essentially masculine. This position obliged Freud to create the concept of the *drive with a passive aim*[10] for feminine sexuality, which raises a certain number of questions on his very vague use of the categories of activity and passivity. We can understand how the energy of the drives might be active, since this energy pushes one to act to satisfy one's goal, but it is hard to see how an *aim* itself can be active or passive. Freud, like so many others in the West, always blindly associates the *active* with the masculine and the *passive* with the feminine, without inquiring as to the origin or the meaning of this conceptual hierarchy.

Does the tenacity of androcentrism stem merely from men's tendencies to dominate, and, from a theoretical point of view, is it linked to the fact that the authors of the great conceptual constructs were men?

I am not sure. Perhaps more profoundly, androcentrism obeys a *metaphysical* fear of division. Thought *in general*, and especially Western thought, experiences a nostalgia for *the one*. The one is thought's resting place; this is where it can stop. The one is desired as an immobile base that assures the closure of wholeness—the wholeness of thought or the wholeness of the world. The one *closes in* on itself.

Division, if it cannot be brought back to an originary unity, is, to the contrary, a structure that *opens*. The two is the gap, the rift, the fatality of the interval and of play. That is why it is difficult to conceive of the origin of a thing or a being as divided, because in the origin we are looking for the completeness of an absolute beginning. In general, the search for the cause, for the origin or the principle of something calls for a simple, single response. The division of the species disturbs this demand for simplicity, and there is always the temptation to reduce the two to the one. Thus, Eve has been made to derive from Adam, man alone has been thought to transmit the germ of life, or it has been assumed that there was only *one sex*, the phallus. The anguish of division, with its perceptible effects on political life, is no doubt not just a matter of sexual difference or its unconscious interpretation. It is linked to the difficulty thought encounters when confronted with difference in general. The metaphysical question is not simply the one posed by Leibniz: "Why is there something rather than nothing?" but also: "Why is reality multiple and not one?"

Accordingly, within the context of sex, division requires us to choose, to choose or to accept being man or woman, to choose to love a man or a woman. These choices are necessarily complicated if we consider that the division of the sexes is always *simultaneously* natural *and* cultural, real *and* symbolic, biological *and* psychic. For each singular existence, division allows for complex figures and contradictions to be drawn. Nevertheless, we cannot escape the primary dichotomy and the dualities it generates.

In fact, we are aware early on of the division of the species. We experience it through our perception of "secondary" sexual characteristics as much as through seeing genital organs or those traits that differentiate genders in our societies. Thus we are registered into the order of this division, we locate ourselves on one side or another. At the same time, the evidence of the "duplicity" of the human nature to which we belong lets us dream of what we could have been, more or less, had we been *on the other side*—and we take pleasure in imagining ourselves as *the other* sex, through thought, cross-dressing, or imitation. Thus, the *other* is not an absolute other but, rather, virtually belongs to my own humanity as part of my possibilities.

Since sexual difference is always and necessarily inscribed in a culture, the meaning it takes on is also dependent upon actual relations between men and women. Thus, there is no hope of one day discovering the *true* nature of difference or the *eternal law* of the relation between the sexes. This difference, at once natural, artificial, and political, cannot be thought of in absolutely neutral* terms. And this is as true in this book as elsewhere. However, it is the awareness of that closure, the recognition of the fact that there is no going beyond that division, that permits an attempt to think about and come to terms with difference.

Thus, each society, in every age, gives its particular version of the universal difference of the sexes. The only constant is the principle of differentiation itself. As for the hierarchy, it has been so destabilized over the past century that it cannot be held as an immutable law, and *difference*, of course, is not necessarily *hierarchy*. The "revolution" that liberated Western women from an ancestral subjugation is certainly the most profound and the most lasting of any of the revolutions that have shaken modern times. This revolution is obviously not over, and we have not yet finished measuring its effects.

It is also because history, as the history of the political relations between the sexes, *has only just begun* that it would be absurd to forget the foundation—the mixed nature of humanity. Up to the present, men have made history and the history of women has unfolded in the margins. It is only today that history is tentatively in the process of becoming mixed.

But let us return to the very nature of mixity itself.

Sexual division forces us to renounce the old dream of a human-

---

*The French *neutre* translated here as "neutral"; it may also be understood as "neuter." *Tr.*

ity derived from *one unique model* and, in its place, to consider a humanity constituted by two distinct human types, simultaneously similar and different. In other words, to think of humanity as *mixed*.

The mixity of "man"—which the French language, as we've already seen, is loath to take into account—is a feature of every society, no matter where it is situated in space and time. Thus the paleontologists have been able to recognize a woman in that little African hominoid who lived more than three million years ago and whom they prettily named Lucy.

This is enough to show that sexual difference is universal, that it is essential to the species as we know it today—and, furthermore, to the species from which we are descended—that it radically transcends different physical human types, whether they are characterized by skin color, facial features, or body morphology. These traits, which account for human beings not having all the same features and for each group valuing its own appearance above others', are fundamentally unstable. The faces of human beings are more or less modified over the course of successive generations. We wanted to classify humans according to certain characteristics in order to better rank them hierarchically. The concept of race, with its ideological uses since the nineteenth century, responds above all to this desire for hierarchical order. Be that as it may, ethnic traits are altogether superficial and accidental compared to sexual difference. We can imagine that one day human beings will present more or less different appearances than those we know today, but it is highly probable that they will still be men or women. That is why it is always the difference of the sexes that serves as a model for all other differences, and the male/female hierarchy that is taken as a metaphor for all inter-ethnic hierarchies.

As evident as this preliminary observation may be, it is easily forgotten. Indeed, women are often spoken of as constituting a particular group, such as "racial" or "ethnic" groups, when not compared to a religious community or a regional population! In France, for some unknown reason, the Corsicans and the Bretons bear the brunt of this comparison, as if the question of women had something in common with questions of regionalism or minorities.

Thus, it is not irrelevant, while thinking tenderly of Lucy, to repeat that women in all times and all countries simply incarnate *humanity* in the same way as men do—without men and women being absolutely identical. Nevertheless, this is what has been denied to women: their equal and different *humanity*.

This denial results from the fact that man has wanted to incarnate the human *alone*, woman being situated at a slight *distance* in relation to man in the generic sense. Not so that she might be a being absolutely *other* than man, no: rather always *less* "man" than him, and thus less *human*. She has always been in the *lesser* position: *socially*, *naturally*, and even *ontologically*. This androcentric way of identifying humanity with men and making minor beings of women, midway between men and children, is nothing new. Ancient Greek culture, as we shall see, provides a striking example.

Sexual difference, I repeat, obeys the principle of the excluded third. There is no more a third sex than there is a sixth sense. As in anatomical illustration plates, *the human figure must be that of a couple*, not a simple figure. That is why, when you want to give *a single face* or *a single name* to the human being, you have to choose between man and woman. Since the human has generally been called *man*, and the original or exemplary man has been represented as a *masculine being*, it was necessary to deploy a great deal of imagination to reinvent woman and explain how she was *not* a man.

One of the greatest weaknesses of abstract universalism is precisely the way it substitutes differentiated human beings with a concept of universal, undifferentiated "man." Naively adopted by a certain branch of feminism, it has allowed for the idea that natural differences must be overcome and cultural differences neutralized. But it goes too far in opposing the universality of the human to the artificial, social "constructions" of the sexes such as they exist in different cultures.

Nevertheless, we often speak of the "social construction" of human subjects constituted as "girls" and "boys," under the pretext that their future status as men and women and their future roles as fathers and mothers has already determined them as girls or boys. Of course, from the moment it involves position and status, the man/woman difference is *always* and *in part* socially constructed. Of course, the statuses of the boy and the girl are necessarily marked by the future society reserves for them. But this future itself could not be socially constructed out of nothing. Nature too, for its part, transforms boys and girls, in a fairly spectacular fashion at the age of puberty, into masculine and feminine beings. Social constructions are not built entirely arbitrarily or autonomously.

What makes the difference between the sexes difficult to define is precisely the impossibility of isolating it from the historical forms it necessarily takes in human societies. This attempt at isolation, comparable to Rousseau's setting off in search of nature,[11] would doubtlessly lead us, like him, to fiction. Why not? Fiction is a part of those interpretations that, in this area as in others, *give meaning* to what is imparted to us and what happens to us.

But the distinction between nature and culture, as conceptually useful as it might be, is not of great help with regard to the difference between the sexes, because nature—always the object of a political, cultural, social, and symbolic reconstruction—conceals itself. If we take off the cultural masks of the sexes, we do not find the true faces of man and woman underneath but another figure, visible elsewhere, or imaginary, of difference. Nor will we discover, under the artifices of gender, a neuter or asexual subject.

Thus we do not have to ask what is the ultimate meaning of difference but understand that all meaning is lodged in differential systems for which sexual mixity is no doubt the principal model.

Rethinking *the mixity of man*—and I expressly use this strange formulation—must then lead to the splitting into two of our representation of the essence of "*man*," in such a way that woman would no longer be a secondary being, that she might experience the pride of being what she is—*woman*—without having to identify herself with the male to appear as fully human. That she might finally be woman, knowing that she *lacks nothing*, except in that she knows the universal finitude of every human being.

Our finitude is revealed through the fact that we are all mortal and sexed, and not through the fact that we are women. . . .

To think about mixity is also to think about the cultural differentiation of natural difference—even if the latter is unknowable. Gender differences constitute possible versions of the natural difference between the sexes and not forms contradicting them. Aristotle explained very well the essential role habit plays for the human being and how much it can be second nature. But if ways of acting can be modified, inflected, and regulated by habit (and thus by culture and its institutions), habit can never entirely contradict nature. You cannot *habituate* a stone from falling when you throw it, nor can you habituate humans to forget that they are sexed, it seems to me, or to no longer desire each other, or to no longer wish to leave behind beings who will survive them. Even before the essential role it plays in all social organization, sexual difference is first and foremost about love, death, and procreation. Marriages, funeral rites, and rules of filiation are essential aspects of every culture. Their variable characteristics should not make us forget that they constitute ways of thinking and experiencing a condition that humans did not choose and that destines humans to love, give birth, and die. These three destinies are inextricable, and they all depend upon our sexed nature.[12]

Gender difference is thus not simply the effect of arbitrary social constructs: it comes to give meaning to this difference of the sexes, which is essential to our condition as mortals.

Societies cultivate sexual difference as one cultivates plants and flowers by producing art and variations in style. To cultivate always means to make grow, to magnify, to exaggerate, and to embellish the natural trait through artifice, just as we make up a face or adorn a body with clothes. Ethnologists often describe how, among certain peoples, it is the men who adorn themselves, and among others, the women, but they also know that, through these choices, difference itself is being signified. More than the traits of one or the other, it is difference being emphasized, adorned, or embellished. There is an art of sexual difference, which takes a thousand forms and gives its characteristics to a society.

On the other hand, in the ideal of a *confusion of the genders*, there is always the dream of an end of art, at the same time—and this is not a contradiction—as a blindness to the natural diversity that inspires it.

Fortunately, under the effect of nature and art, difference always returns. So adeptly that, within communities seeking to achieve a sort of homogeneity, a duality of traits, characteristics, behaviors is reconstituted. From the beginning of time, cross-dressing has been used to represent gender difference, to mimic, both among men and among women, the division of one into two. Every society plays at differentiating the sexes, and, when difference is uncertain or absent—for example in unmixed groups—it is reintroduced or caricatured. This shows that nostalgia for the one does not exclude a taste for the multiple.

Is it even possible to imagine a uniform humanity, in harmony with itself and not dual, not in disaccord? No, and if we believe we have achieved this, we are struck with terror and boredom at imagining beings so similar they understand each other immediately. It seems that, without sexual difference, differences between individuals would not suffice to render them opaque to each other. They would surely harmonize too well, and this absence of *others* would be a hell. That is why I am not among those who dream of erasing differences, or standardizing men's and women's life styles, or even, in the end, of absolutely equalizing their conditions, if this means the suppression of all dissymetry in behavior. Certainly, in the final analysis, it is the irreplaceable singularity of beings that counts, but this singularity itself is composed of certain traits, among which figures the signifier of sex.

VERSİO⊙ΠS ⊙F DİFFEREΠCE

It was said of Cézanne that he was "imaginative *in front of* things."[1]
I suppose that, in general, human imagination works that way: it
imagines the real. This is at least one possible way of conceiving
these cultural *folds* of which I spoke earlier.

Thus the natural difference of the sexes is only the enigmatic
"starting point" for the infinite deployment of meanings that the
difference of *genders* takes on in all aspects of social life. Nature
gives the *two*; cultures invent a multiplicity of possible variations of
this duality. Humans are very imaginative in front of the sexes. The
very multiplicity of these *versions of difference* indicates that they
are the fruit of original creations.

Consequently, one must not confuse *reference* to the natural reality of the sexes with *submission* to a natural order. Nature inspires
us, but the abundance of symbolic forms and social structures of
the duality of kinds demonstrates a diversity of translations we'd
have to call free, since no one translation is any more accurate than
another. There are only versions of difference, with no original ver-

sion. Versions, translations, interpretations: all of these words express an action giving meaning and value, a gesture without which sexual difference would remain meaningless.

Many versions or *expressions* of difference exist: political expressions related to the distribution of power, aesthetic expressions treating the *figuration* of the sexes and the representations of masculine and feminine, economic expressions implying a sexual division of labor. And still others. The multiplicity of these expressions and their great variety through space and time permits us to think they express nothing immutable, if not difference itself and its relation to birth and death. Like all sexed beings, the human individual is destined to die and survives as a species only by "reproducing" itself (as we so wrongly put it, since individuals are not all identical). Beyond the psychological, sociological, or political questions, sexual difference comes back to only one issue, the one linking birth and death. I am speaking here of death as biological fate, the death biologists link to sexual reproduction—both of them belong to the same "logic of the living." This is why we cannot separate the meaning and value of sexual difference from the question of generation, even if expressions of difference lead us well beyond the domain of reproduction, toward politics.

Natural difference, in its essential connection with birth, says nothing to us about the way in which relations between men and women find themselves concretely regulated. These relations are conventional; they result simultaneously from power struggles and negotiations, and they are thus political. Although very real, natural differences never directly engender social or cultural norms. The norm is always moral, political, and aesthetic.

Thus there is always a *politics of the sexes*, that is, a necessity for each of the sexes to advance a politics, consciously or not, because there is no *truth of the sexes*, no absolute knowledge of sexual difference, and thus no correct or obvious way to give it a definitive status. At best, there is *play* and there are *stakes*, difficult relations to negotiate, which involve power struggles and from which no one is exempt. There is no position of advantage, no possibility for arbitration. All of us, men and women, are thus committed to strategies that take into account, as do all strategies, the other's calculations, the other's desires and interests.

Unless one of the two sexes wished to and could survive without the other—which perhaps the mastery of cloning will permit—the game is programmed, inevitable. Each sex can only measure its strengths, endlessly negotiate its positions, determine its politics as best it can.

However, the political nature of this relationship has only really appeared quite recently, because the natural givens and the power struggles have, until now, favored Kate Millett's "Politics of the Male."[2]

To speak of a politics of the sex*es*, in the plural, is, rather, to emphasize the need for both sexes to become conscious of a certain closure to the scene where male/female relations are played out and also of the fact that this game seems to have no end.

The political nature of the male/female relation does not open up the prospect of an ultimate emancipation or peace. Rather, this politicization marks the *inevitability (fatalité) of eternal discord*. Without this originary discord, human relations would be deprived of their first enigma, their first doubt about the identity of the other and the problem forever posed by coexistence with him—or her. Uncertainty and misunderstanding are the motivating forces in relations between the sexes, for the first anthropoids, no doubt, as for Marivaux's characters. There had to be a breach, there had to be a *game*, in order to invent rules, ruses, compromises.

Now the game does not derive solely from a natural difference but from conflicts of interest and mutual dependence. Men and women depend on each other for the satisfaction of their desires as well as for procreation. Many other disputes follow. We aren't likely to ever get beyond them, and we shouldn't complain about them.

In certain respects, it might be considered that the ideal of the reduction of difference or, as it's called, the "*disappearance of genders*," would constitute a totalitarian fantasy in aiming for a uniformization of individuals. There is nothing worse than the dream of a society of like individuals liberated from conflicts by their very likeness. What is often called "the end of ideologies"—and that is more precisely only the end of ideologies *of the end*—signifies that we have ceased to believe that struggles and conflicts—indeed wars—could and should have an end, and that, if this end is attained, they would stop. We have ceased to hope for permanent peace with justice realized and freedom achieved. We no longer believe in the final liberation of men or women nor in the lasting resolution of the conflicts between them. In this sense *we are departing from the feminism* that subscribed to modern theories of liberation. But we can only depart from it because this feminism has prevailed with regard to the essentials, at least in Western civilization, since women have become conscious of the fact that they are responsible for their own destinies, that they must think about and fulfill them.

Conscious that we can transcend *neither* differences *nor* disputes, we must now develop a way to think about universality that doesn't lean to one side or the other but allows humanity its mixity and thus its internal alterity.

By *versions of difference*, I do not mean simply institutional forms that relations between the sexes have historically taken on but also the mythological and theoretical forms that have provided diverse interpretations of sexual difference through representations or conceptual systems.

Theories of difference, just like myths, have always been political theories, that is, instruments of politics—conservative or transformative as the case may be.

The "subjection of women," according to the formulation of John Stuart Mill,[3] has no doubt been as universal as sexual difference. All over, and in a variety of forms, relations between the sexes appear as distinctly hierarchized, and men have established their power—at the same time as they legitimize it—on mythological, religious, ideological, or scientific grounds. The foundations of power in general were hardly called into question before the Enlightenment, much less the foundations of masculine power. Thus it is not astonishing that women have so rarely sought to determine for themselves their place and status. They have shaped themselves to the familial, economic, political, and religious orders instituted by those who have held the monopoly on power. An ancestral patriarchy has continually sustained the real power of men based on the idea of a supposedly *natural* subordination of women. Naturalist theories have always contributed to the establishment and founding of the political order. But, as we well know, the "natural" order is always permeated with the *political use* we wish to put it to. What we are given, and this is no small thing, is immediately interpreted and evaluated.

Aristotle thus elaborated a *hierarchical* theory of natural sexual difference running through all areas where this difference is expressed—in particular the "biological," with the roles of masculine and feminine in generation, and the political, with the place of men and women in the *polis*. He affirms, for example, that the male alone plays an active role in generation because he alone provides the semen, that is, the generative principle, while the female only provides the material for the future embryo.[4] In his *Politics*, he bases the institution of the family on the "natural" superiority of man, the dominant element, and on the inferiority of woman, the subordinate element, declaring that "every family is governed in monarchistic form by the eldest male."[5] To speak of "monarchistic" form with regard to the family seems metaphorical, since Aristotle normally reserves this term to describe a type of political structure in the strictest sense. Nevertheless, and the place of the family at the very beginning of Aristotle's text proves this, Aristotelian politics could exclude neither the family nor women, insofar as, within the family, both authority and law are at stake. The family is a small monarchistic community entirely commanded by the father. As is often the case in Aristotle, the poet's words comes to pronounce a truth lost in the mists of time, and here, it is Homer who provides the principle: "Each one dictates the law to his children and to his wives."[6]

Such is the knot tying the natural to the political. The "natural" superiority of the male requires him to "dictate the law," that is, to institute a political order. If we continue reading these famous pages where Aristotle writes that "man is by nature a political animal," we realize that the aptitude for political life is given to human beings *with the word*. Indeed, it is because they can say "the useful and the harmful," because they can say "the just and the unjust" that humans, as opposed to animals, share the sense of good and evil and create families and city-states.[7] This beautiful remark on the word as condition for the possibility of politics awakens a suspicion on the part of the reader, and even more so on the part of the female reader, who asks herself if the human, in its feminine version, truly has the capacity to "speak." Because if indeed she does, she should be equally capable of saying the just and the unjust, and it no longer makes sense that men have the right to "dictate the law" to women.

Thus we must admit that, in some way, woman *cannot speak*. Either by nature, or because, according to men's laws, it is not right for her to speak, to say the law. By positing women and children as the primary objects of the law, Aristotle seems to found the familial hierarchy on a natural hierarchy. But, as woman is perfectly capable of speaking, and elsewhere Aristotle affirms that man and woman are both free, we might suspect that woman's silence is far less natural than political.

Indeed, men's governments respond more to political demand than to natural necessity. It is the master/slave relationship that explicitly refers to a difference between "he whose nature is to command and he whose nature is to be commanded."[8] While the interests of the familial community require that it be governed by only one person, Aristotle was so sure that male authority was not absolutely self-evident that he invoked a hierarchical principle more obvious and more natural than sexual difference: age difference. If the male serves as a guide for the female, it is also because the husband is traditionally older than his wife: "The older and fully developed being is destined to command the younger and imperfect being."[9] The "permanent inequality" at the heart of the conjugal community depends less upon woman's essential inferiority than upon the familial institution itself, which unites a mature, adult man with a young, inexperienced woman. Thus Aristotle logically considers the husband's authority over his wife to be a political power, different from the master/slave relationship that, according to him, is grounded entirely in nature.

In the history of theory on sexual difference, we nearly always encounter the family as the structure within which the subordination of women is established. Aristotle's merit is to have understood and demonstrated the political nature of that institution. The institutional order takes advantage of nature more than it follows from it in linking the husband's authority over his wife with the age difference between them. The places and roles of men and women are not defined by nature but institutionalized according to the functions each must carry out in to ensure the survival and continuation of the family. Thus Aristotle is much less a naturalist than is often believed and much more political.

It seems quite tricky to decide if the definition according to which "man is by nature a political animal" should only be *understood* in the masculine version of *anthropos*. In this case, the male would by nature have a monopoly over the word and power and woman would naturally obey. But if, generally, all humans are political animals, and if, as Aristotle reminds us, man and woman are both free beings, the silence and obedience of the woman in marriage might already be the effect of political consent on her part. I am inclined toward this second interpretation, conforming to the idea of the family as first political community, site of the emergence of the law and institutionalized power relationships.

This Aristotelian conception of the family, despite its eminently phallocratic character, and insofar as it admits the political nature of the man/woman relation in marriage, is more open than it might seem, in that it allows for the possibility of transforming the institution. If woman is by nature free, and if she is also a political animal, nothing prevents the possibility that one day she too will be able to find the voice to "say the just and the unjust" rather than just listening to the law dictated to her.

This is, in fact, what she has done. Thus the law is no longer only the affair of men. And one may predict that, in the future, women and men will together treat the affairs of the city-state.

Let us draw from this analysis of the family that nature is not the basis for political order but that a political strategy always "works on" a theory of nature. This strategy is not only at work in the field of political theory but already in the fields of the natural and social sciences. Concern with the hierarchization of the two sexes was also expressed by Aristotle in his *Histoire des animaux* and in his treatise *De la Génération des animaux*.[10] Furthermore, this hierarchy is applied, by analogy, to the fundamental concepts of metaphysics, as when the philosopher announces that "matter aspires to the Form just as the female desires the male."

Thus sexual difference never seems to present itself directly, in its crude state, as it were. It always manifests itself through an interpretation that has already inscribed the masculine/feminine couple into a hierarchy. This appears even more clearly in comparing the Aristotelian version of sexual difference and a theoretical version very far removed from it, such as Freud's—as far removed in time as in point of view, since it is a question of natural history in one instance and psychology in the other.

We should note, however, and this is what interests me, that even while relying upon totally different "facts," *these two versions arise from the same logic*: the binary logic that opposes one to zero, presence to absence, and the masculine sex organ to its privation—feminine castration. In both cases, it is obvious that woman *lacks* something man has, and, in both cases, the theoretician acts as if this lack is a matter of a simple empirical assertion.

The following, however, must be considered. For Aristotle, woman (and females in general) is deprived of the heat that would give her the capacity to procreate. She is incapable of producing a seed, and through a sort of cooking process, of making it "take Form." Only the male can be considered as fertile because he produces the seed that will transmit the essence of the species to the embryo. Aeschylus had already written: "It is not the mother who gives birth to what we call her child: she only nurses the germ sown in her. The one who gives birth is the man who impregnates her."[11]

We see that Jean-Pierre Vernant was not forcing an interpretation when he wrote that the "dream of a purely paternal heredity never stopped haunting the Greek imagination."[12] This dream was even more profound and more potent than the Platonic contempt for procreation.

By relying solely on the role of each sex in reproduction and opposing man's procreative power to woman's lack thereof, the Aristotelian theory of sexual difference leads to a thinking of femininity as *privation* and a generalized description of the female as a *mutilated male*.

A comparison with the Freudian theory of sexual difference reveals a similar logic. While the Aristotelian feminine mutilation was due to a lack of heat, and thus of semen, Freudian castration is due, for the child who has made the discovery, to the lack of a penis among girls. Beginning from a completely different choice of criteria, the emission of semen in one case, the anatomy of genital organs in the other, the same structuring of difference within the *presence/absence* opposition appears. We must stress that the choice of differential elements, which are not at all of the same order, seems to go without saying in both cases, while one might just as well point to other criteria, such as breasts or the ability to carry children. It's rather strange to suppose that children discover sexual difference through the anatomy of other children, as if the anatomy of adults were not immediately much more visible (a woman's breasts in particular) or as if a multitude of other attributes had not already placed this difference before the child's gaze. It is manifestly arbitrary to reduce the perception that children might initially have of sexual difference to the sight of the genital organs. From the point of view of ordinary experience, for children as for adults, the perception of genders—masculine or feminine—and of the distinction between men and women always precedes the sight of the anatomical sex. "Secondary" sexual characteristics—general morphology and even vocal quality—are perceived as signifying sexual difference well before the discovery of the genital organs.

If we pursue this comparison between these two theories, we notice that both fail to question the choice of differential elements. Everything takes place as if these elements were obvious, immediate givens. It is true that psychoanalysis, with anatomical difference, relies on visible elements, while Aristotle speaks of more hidden things. In fact, the penis is visible. It is even, according to Freud, particularly apparent to the gaze of the child, who sees nothing *in the place of the penis* in the little girl. As for the Greek philosopher, he must develop a complex argumentation, and for good reason, in order to make apparent the exact location of woman's lack. But the result of the two "descriptions" is the same: the differentiation of the species into two sexes is substituted either for a unique masculine model from which woman more or less deviates and which she cannot transmit, or for a sole visible sex organ, the penis, and a sole sexual signifier, the phallus. Lacan, who knows quite well that these anatomical considerations are rather secondary in relation to the androcentric order, nonetheless justifies the choice of the phallus as privileged signifier because it is "the most salient of what can be captured in the real of sexual copulation." He also invokes the turgidity of the masculine sex, the "image of vital flux" that passes in reproduction, to legitimate the primacy of the phallus, while simultaneously distancing himself from the Freudian scene.[13]

Beginning from the child's gaze at the only sexual organ considered visible, the boy and the girl will thus be confronted, according to Freud, with, for one, the anguishing possibility of castration, and for the other, the "discovery" of her own castration.

There is, of course, no question of assimilating the theories of Aristotle and Freud since their fields and objects are not the same.

The *Generation of Animals*, deals with the biological question of procreation, while the famous article "Several Psychic Consequences of the Anatomical Differences of the Sexes"[14] treats the relationship between anatomy and the psyche. But beginning from profoundly different historical and scientific contexts, the structure of masculine/feminine difference is still interpreted through the opposition between a thing's presence and its absence. The choice of differential traits seems relatively secondary in relation to the general meaning given to difference. What is essential, in each instance, is the primacy of the masculine and the definition of the feminine as lack, privation, and impotence.

Might one not see in the persistence of this structure the proof of its universality? And isn't sexual difference to be understood as an essential dissymetry? But neither difference nor dissymetry need necessarily be interpreted as a logic of lack. In its substitution of *one* for *two* (*l'un aux deux*), this logic is metaphysical. In its placement of the masculine at the center, it is political.

The hierarchization of difference is not merely the effect of its inscription in a binary system. If the sexual alternative places us well within a *binary* logic (*either* masculine *or* feminine), this logic is not necessarily a *logic of lack*, opposing one term to its absence. To the contrary, the binary structure formulated via the disjunction "a" *or* "not-a," or again, "one" *or* "zero," poses a hierarchy between positive and negative, presence and absence. "Phallocentrism" is a product of this structure in opposing the phallus to its lack and phallic virility to castrated femininity. This logic of lack must be replaced with a logic of difference, but a difference without hierarchy that I will term a *logic of the mixed*.

The mixed structure also poses an alternative, but it does not hierarchize this alternative. Sexual difference is indeed a dichotomy, and it also logically resembles a disjunction, since every individual is masculine *or* feminine—"a" *or* "b." But this disjunction only signifies that *either* "a" *or* "b" is true, and thus that "a" *and* "b" cannot both be true at the same time. This does not mean that one of the terms is positive and the other negative, that one is simply the negation of the other. More precisely, there is indeed, logically, a double negation: feminine is not masculine, and masculine is not feminine. But, if only one of the two negations is retained, the alternative is centered on one of the two terms. For example: woman is not a man. This is how androcentric logic functions. If one placed women at the center or at the summit of humanity, one would say: men are not women, designating the masculine as lack.

The logic of the mixed posits that the human is necessarily masculine *or* feminine, that there is a double version of "man," without one version being inferior to the other. This logic posits that a woman *is not a man* (which has always been said), but, in addition, that a man is this individual *who is not a woman* (which has been said far less often). Thus, the sexual alternative is not played out between that which is *present* or *absent*, unless in the sense that the lack is double. Each of the two is deprived of that which the other has or is.

According to this perspective, there is, so to speak, no unilateral castration, if you could call it that. In one sense, sexual difference leaves behind the logic of lack. In another, it suggests the idea of a double castration. Neither man nor woman constitutes "the whole human."

Taking into account, however, the fact that the sexual alternative applies to everyone, one might situate lack on the side of the metaphysical subject who denies the alternative. The *neuter subject*, in some sense angelic and beyond sex, a prelapsarian being, this figure attests to a dream of "purity," philosophical as much as religious. Because it cannot overcome the division of the human, this dream—

or in other words, the anguish of mixity—will always remain rooted in a fantasy of a single, and not a double, humanity. But since this dream of simplicity has no model, it can only be represented by *one of the two sexes*. The misapprehension of mixity always replaces the two with *one* of the two.

Freud's theoretical superiority does not lie in his presentation of lack as an objective reality but, rather, in his thinking of lack as the effect of an unconscious interpretation of anatomical difference. Freud knows quite well that one is always, inevitably, engaged in interpretation. Nevertheless, from the moment this interpretation is given as universal, it becomes a rule and even a norm that Freud fails to call into question. For Freud, women must accept their difference and renounce their envy of the penis they lack.

Now, and it is here that the theory reveals its political stakes, for Freud, "penis envy" is expressed in women through the desire to act *like men* and to have the same social ambitions as men! This transference of penis envy onto ambition suggests a necessary and natural relation between sexual difference and individuals' social and professional functions. We had to wait for Karen Horney[15] and Melanie Klein for psychoanalysis to pose the question of knowing whether the place and the status of men in the social and cultural order might not provoke women's desire to be men as much as, if not more than, the unique fact of having a penis. Freud finds it inherently natural that one must be a man, and thus have a penis, to exercise certain social functions. Ambition, for him, is normally masculine. Freud remains very conservative on this point because he still believes in an immutable social destiny for women. Ambition in women remains for him the expression of her desire to be a man—and thus of her "penis envy"—but he is unable to suppose that, inversely, a woman's ambition, in society such as it is (and even more as it was at the beginning of the twentieth century), provokes her desire to be a man. And provokes *in addition*, I might add, penis envy. . . . On this point, Simone de Beauvoir was right on the mark: "The covetous desire on the girl's part, when it appears, results from a preexisting valorization of virility: Freud takes it for granted when it must be accounted for."[16]

But the *political* dimension of Freud is limited neither to its traditionalism in terms of the distribution of roles in social life nor even to the psychoanalytic interpretation of anatomical difference. As we have just seen, the political dimension begins with the anatomical description itself, with the choice of the penis as the *sole signifier of sex*. From the outset, in order to "describe" difference, this theory chooses the trait *woman lacks*. The rest follows: castration, penis envy, child as *substitute* for the penis, etc.

However, the critiques of phallocentrism devoted to asserting early knowledge of the vagina, contesting penis envy and demonstrating the representation of the feminine sex from childhood on, have perhaps been misguided. This point of view subscribed to the very logic it contested in seeking a "feminine equivalent" of the penis—that is, in accepting the anatomy of genital organs as the primary criterion for the representation of the sexes (with the conscious and unconscious consequences this entails). The debate opposing the visibility of the penis and the invisibility of the vagina was already a trap. From the moment when *the locus of the sexual signifier* had been situated in the penis (or in any masculine feature), feminine *lack* followed. We must go much further toward a recognition of difference and, thus, dissymetry. It is not *from one* that we must describe *the other*, or we privilege one of the two terms; we immediately hierarchize difference and remain within the logic of lack. On the contrary, we must locate a set of differential elements, including fecundity and the role of procreation, which are no less important than anatomy for the representation of the sexes and its conscious and unconscious psychic effects. That dolls, so well-loved by girls *in general*, and no matter what might be said, appear as penis substitutes rather than baby or child substitutes is an example of a kind of theoretical acrobatics that must be questioned and that bears witness to the androcentrism of the psychoanalytic order.

Here again, it is not simply the theoretician's sex that must be challenged but a philosophical difficulty in conceiving and defining difference *as such*. Because a difference is never itself seen, is not *presented* in *one of the two*, difference signifies the in-between and the gap. There is no *place*, no assigned placement for difference, only a way, for each of the two sexes for example, to be *otherwise* than the other one. If difference is nowhere, we cannot think about it by beginning from one element but, rather, by considering the play of elements, their relationships.

The androcentric, or phallocentric, structure, is always associated with other conceptual couples, also hierarchized, that qualify and reinforce the masculine/feminine opposition. This is the case, for example, with the active/passive couple: no matter which differential traits are retained to describe sexual difference, the masculine is always "active," while the "passive" qualifies the feminine— at least in the Western tradition. Thus, in Aristotle, for example, the male generative principle is *active* and the nourishing matter *passive*. In the Freudian field, it is the sexual energy of the drives that is active, because this energy prompts action in order to satisfy the drives (*les pulsions*). The libido is by nature male, and this renders feminine desire very enigmatic.

Would it be less apt to consider the desire to bear children and feminine fecundity determinant elements of sexuality and thus to wonder if men do not also define themselves through their incapacity to give birth? Couldn't this impotence create in him an over-estimation of his sex and penis worship as a substitute for the child he cannot carry? The theory of lack can always be inverted, and a primary way of deconstructing the traditional hierarchy consists in operating this inversion of negative and positive definitions. This is Antoinette Fouque's move when she writes: "To be born man is in large part to feel oneself excluded from giving birth."[17]

In this way one might oppose the absolute value of feminine fecundity to phallocentrism and completely reverse the traditional oppositions. It would be tempting to think that the Greek dream of a purely "paternal heredity" constitutes a symptom of the masculine *envy* of fecundity. It has been proposed, for example, that the Greek myths of *autochthony* that would have Athenian citizens born from the very ground of the fatherland (*auto-chtôn*) have as their effect, as Nicole Loraux demonstrates, the supplanting of the parental couple and the effacement of Mother Earth to the profit of *fathers' earth.*[18]

The question of difference and the androcentric response always bring us back to the mystery of birth. One might recognize in the Christian myth of the incarnation a way of establishing a purely paternal, direct, and mysterious filiation between God the Father and his Son. But the role of the Virgin Mary intervenes both to permit and prevent this filiation. She permits it, since, as a virgin, she gives birth outside any sexual relation, thus without a father. The Father, who "sends" a son to Mary, engenders without a woman. The incarnation thus takes place outside the relation between two sexes: on one side, a father/son relation without woman; on the other, a mother/son relation without man. The Christian myth of the incarnation, with Mary's maternity, thus establishes a strange compromise. Christ is indeed born of a father and a mother, but without there having been any relation between them. The mystery of filiation, of birth, intersects with the mystery of the relation—or nonrelation—between the sexes. As Hubert Damisch says with regard to the *Madonna del Parto*, the superb and enigmatic image of the pregnant Virgin, the figure of Mary is at the transitional moment between "Holy History and individual experience."[19]

But reversals of perspective do not necessarily result in a "gynocentric" position—the very word is barbarous—that is, a position that displaces humanity's *center* toward the feminine side. One would then remain in the same metaphysical logic—the logic of the same: the occultation of the two (*du deux*) to the benefit of the *one* (*l'un*): negation of difference to the benefit of the oppositions of presence/absence, activity/passivity, visible/invisible, etc.; a forgetting of the mixed structure to the benefit of a hierarchy. The reversal of the hierarchy vindicates women and shows that lack is also on the other side—so many actions with political and theoretical utility must still be pursued.

This is neither sufficient nor satisfactory philosophically. Binary logic and the hierarchies it institutes cannot be truly overcome unless we renounce the center in general, the desire for a center, and the desire that there be the *one* before the *two*, the single before the double. The thinking of sexual duality requires us to remain within difference, that is, in the in-between. It requires us to think about alterity without wanting it to return to the same—or to a single—identity. Thus: a renunciation of the logic of the center and the metaphysics of presence so that we might dare to affront this irreducible difference mixity suggests.[20]

Indeed, mixity designates a purely differential structure in which neither of the two terms is derived from the other. The *two* never derives from the *one* but, rather, the *one* always derives from the *two* of those who engendered the individual. However, this individual does not in any way exceed or "supersede" the originary sexual difference, he renews it in himself in being either *the male one of the two—or the female one of the two*—and not the unification of the two. The individual himself is traversed by difference, always avoiding aspirations to a single unity.

Nevertheless, everything leads to the realization that a nostalgia for the *one* haunts us and, without deciding whether this nostalgia is of a biological or metaphysical order, I will say that it is expressed through an anguish with regard to division and consequently an *anguish with regard to mixity*. Because if humanity is mixed, and not single, all individuals are confronted with their own insufficiency and cannot fully claim to be full human beings.

Each sex is thus "mutilated," or insufficient, and each sex knows the castration of not being the other. There is indeed a *lack essential to every human being*, which is neither the lack of a penis nor some other attribute of men, or women, but stems from being only male or only female. The consciousness of this originary privation has nothing to do with the myth of a lost completeness—each one being half of an initially full and total being—because this myth also refers back to a primary undifferentiated identity. To the contrary, such a consciousness implies the recognition of an originary division.

Most theories of sexual difference have attempted to reduce the mixity of the species through the subordination of the other to the one, the suppression of the dizziness brought on by the *two* through reference to a unique center. We can do no more than to propose a new theoretical version of difference, one which is both philosophical and political in its attempt to break with the nostalgia of the one.

FREEDO⊙M AND FECUNDITY

At this point the difference between sex, as a natural characteristic, and the politics of the sexes, as the freedom to interpret difference and regulate the relations between the sexes, should let us avoid entering into a useless and deceptive struggle with nature. It is not because a very old masculine discourse has called upon nature to legitimate its empire that we must again challenge and consider that an actual natural "inferiority" is at the origin of the history of women's condition.

In this regard, it is time to break with the logic of *The Second Sex*, which has conceived the emancipation of women only as a refusal of sexual identity, relegated to the order of contingency to the benefit of the ideal of a universal identity whereby difference would disappear. At least this was Simone de Beauvoir's reasoning in the era of the book that made her the principal theoretician of feminism—and that was decisive for generations of women, from the beginning of the fifties to the present.

If I speak here of "breaking," it is because I am one of those women for whom *The Second Sex* opened up a true perspective on liberation. Consequently, I have felt all the more strongly its limits and impasses, in particular when I understood that the freedom extolled by the philosopher is paid for by an absurd denial of nature, of maternity, and of the feminine body in general—a constant source of a "carnal alienation" experienced as much in eroticism as in maternity.

The liberating effects of *The Second Sex* were fairly considerable, notably through the emphasis placed on the need for economic independence. The author deserves considerable recognition, inasmuch as her work still continues to manifest an incredible audacity as a result of both her freedom of tone and her frank and raw way of speaking about sexual life and its relation to social life. The necessary immodesty of this book, which caused quite a scandal at the time, has made its author an example of intellectual courage; it has liberated generations of women and will continue to do so in the future.

But this should not preclude a radical calling into question of one of the principal dimensions of de Beauvoir's feminism, namely the desire to efface *women's difference*[1] through the exclusive valorization of virile values and the adoption of masculine models. The effacement of difference has been effected at the price of a new abasement of the feminine in association with the devalorization of the attributes of maternity. As we shall see, the shame of the feminine has haunted feminism.

According to Simone de Beauvoir, civilization has kept women in subordinate situations because, for the most part, they have been condemned to dedicate themselves to the reproduction of the species. An "object" employed by men, woman could only liberate herself through assuming, like men, an existence as a free "subject," by becoming capable of acting in the world and inventing her own goals. The means of erasing differences of condition was only possible through the effacement of natural differences. It was above all a question of affirming the identity of all human beings beyond sexual differences.

However, at the very moment when, at the end of the forties, and better than anyone else, Simone de Beauvoir grasped all of the pitfalls of the feminine condition, most notably that of economic alienation, she did not see her own condition, that is, her philosophical alienation. This consisted especially in the renewal of the masculine/feminine hierarchy as such, along with its associated oppositions: subject and object, activity and passivity.

Indeed, not only does the author of *The Second Sex* fail to criticize the classic description of sexual difference but she sustains it *as is*, as if woman had, logically in the end, suffered from a natural handicap linked to her body and its "biological function."[2] The feminine body is constantly described as a burden of flesh enclosing woman in either an erotic or a childbearing passivity and turning her into an object, an instrument of masculine activity and desire. Whether caressed or penetrated, woman passively undergoes the amorous relation: "She feels that she is an instrument: liberty rests wholly with the other."[3] But never does the author wonder precisely what the active/passive opposition means, nor even whether activity is necessarily synonymous with freedom. Above all, she admits that feminine fecundity has constituted a major obstacle to women's freedom, even though this theme plays a part in the most classic phallocratic argumentation.

There is, in fact, *no reason* why fecundity, which constitutes the principal characteristic differentiating women from men, represents a handicap and "justifies" marginalizing women within oppressive structures. There is no reason; rather, it is the effect of an *interpretive violence* practiced by the other sex and associated with a *de facto domination*. The two always go together. Natural feminine fecundity cannot, a priori and in general, be qualified as a *disadvantage* in relation to masculine individuals since it also grants women the considerable power of providing descendants to both sexes. This power has also given women a great value.

Before stopping at what women may have lacked, we should attempt to understand the crucial mission with which they have been charged, not only by the will of men but also, no doubt, by their own aspirations. The ambition to carry the future of a family, a tribe, a people was not necessarily foreign to women. The valorization of childbirth could not have been merely the effect of a calculation on the part of men to confine mothers.

Nothing proves that a woman can only be free through the denial of one of her most beautiful and gratifying possibilities. Think of those feminine biblical figures traditionally called "matriarchs." They are not simply mothers, they are the "mothers of Israel," and they thereby achieve an exceptional status.[4] Peace between the sexes certainly does not reign in the Old Testament where the ancestral stake of the sexual relation, legal or illegal, with or without marriage is always the child. In the Old Testament, women, like men, are shown in a state of obvious interdependence, faced with one major concern: that of descendants.

We often suppose that woman, as mother, is used and made an instrument by man. But we forget that the concern with descendants does not belong exclusively to men. From this point of view, the "instrumentality" is necessarily reciprocal, and the question of knowing which one uses the other, which one makes a means or an instrument of the other, is not easily decidable. This is confirmed today, now that procreative and contraceptive techniques have given women control over their own reproduction. Nietzsche writes in *The Gay Science* that for a woman "man is only a means: the end is always the child." This provocative affirmation is in the process of coming true, women ultimately choosing with which man and at what moment they will have children. In the past women have always used their power to be mothers—and their powers *as* mothers. But this mastery and these powers remained limited, while, we may suppose, man's uncertainty with regard to paternity, like his incapacity to completely master the process of conception, constituted a handicap that led him to appropriate one or more women to provide him with descendants (and to attempt to assure himself that they were truly his own).

This is the hypothesis of Françoise Héritier, who sees the traditional hierarchy of the sexes as the effect of men's desire to control reproduction. Her hypothesis seems far more pertinent—and less marked by a masculine reading of history—than Simone de Beauvoir's, which holds onto the idea that fertility constitutes a natural handicap and element of inferiority. De Beauvoir's vision corresponds with the internalization of a dominating masculine ideology. Feminine fecundity seems, to the contrary, a natural power that masculine and feminine strategies strive to master.

In this respect our time represents an essential phase in the liberation of women, since, for the first time, women are becoming fully responsible for this extraordinary power to give life, reversing the traditional androcentric legal order. Not too long ago in France, every child born to a married woman was ascribed to her husband. Now it is women who control both birth and filiation. This revolution, which would have been difficult to anticipate in the nineteen-forties, explains *in part* why nature used to seem like a major obstacle to freedom. Fertility was already a force, and many women experienced it as such, but this poorly mastered force entered into contradiction with other forms of freedom. In this sense, the claim to breaking with nature found its justification.

We must regret, however, that Simone de Beauvoir, as she argues from the first pages of *The Second Sex*, remained dependent upon Sartre's concept of freedom and situated herself "within the perspective of the existentialist code,"[5] because this code uses and abuses the opposition between nature and freedom.

Existentialist philosophy is indeed the heir to a *dualistic* metaphysics that, since Plato, has opposed *the soul to the body, the intelligible to the sensible*, and—a more recent opposition—*culture to nature*. Now, these oppositions maintain an essential relationship to sexual difference and its hierarchization. While the questions here are very complex and cannot be analyzed quickly, it may be said that classical conceptual hierarchies always serve to give meaning to masculine/feminine difference and that, inversely, this difference metaphorically expresses metaphysical oppositions (as when Aristotle explains that "matter aspires to form just as the the female desires the male"). In this tradition, femininity—always associated with the body, sensitivity, and nature—is thus metaphysically devalued. But, to escape this logic, it would be necessary to contest the very principle of these simplistic oppositions. Among the most decisive on the subject, let us refer back to the opposition of activity to passivity and of subject to object, which play such a major role in Sartre's analyses of freedom.

Freedom, in its existentialist incarnation, is essentially the subject's ability to act and thereby *transcend* his condition, and first and foremost, his *natural* condition. This idea has a long history and can be found in all of the Kantians and neo-Kantians. But this freedom, which derives its philosophical origins from the idea of free will and, in our time, takes on the figure of the gratuitous act (all the more free in that it has neither motive nor reason), is only a partial conceptualization of freedom. This freedom is essentially negativity, the power to say no, in all the forms this *no* might take. This freedom presupposes a rigid opposition between necessity and freedom, immanence and transcendence, and, according to Sartre's vocabulary, the *in-itself* and the *for-itself* (in other words, between the being that is only what it is, as a simple object, and the consciousness that chooses itself freely, the true subject).

As might have been foreseen, once the general analogy between philosophical hierarchies and the masculine/feminine difference has been posited, existentialism enacts a sexual redistribution of concepts: for men, freedom and the innate power to continuously transcend themselves; for women, the natural tendency to let themselves to be confined in immanence and to be treated as objects by men. We can thus understand women's particular difficulty in conquering their freedom.

Indeed, as paradoxical as it may seem, for the author of *The Second Sex*, men and women are not created altogether equal in the face of human freedom. Despite the apparent universality of the concept of the *subject*, woman is less naturally a *subject* than man, in the valorized sense of this concept, as opposed to the concept of the *object*. Reading Simone de Beauvoir, we notice that men and women are not equally active. Man seems to be born active and as a subject (which are the same thing). He spontaneously transcends his given reality, while the biological destiny of woman relegates her to passivity, and she will only be able to become a truly active and free subject through the elimination of her original passivity. To the extent that the creative active mode is somehow natural in men—

who, since *homo faber*, realize themselves as existing through their projects—so too does the "absurd fecundity of woman"* prevent her, at least originally, from "active participation in the increase of these resources."[6] The ideal of existentialist freedom is associated here with the valorization of work and the modernist ideology of productivity. Insofar as it represents the highest form of activity and transforms the real—in other words, transcends and negates it—work is a privileged expression of freedom. Again, inasmuch as it produces objects as the result of a project, it freely transcends immediate reality and objectively manifests, in the world, the subject's actions.

Fecundity does not really have a place in the modern value system. It neither fabricates merchandise nor increases resources. And more seriously: it is not an "activity" and thus gives women no experience of freedom: "giving birth and breast-feeding are not *activities*, they are natural functions; no project is involved; and that is why woman found in them no reason for a lofty affirmation of her existence—she submits passively to her biological fate"[7] All this is problematic: the absence of a project, the lack of activity—passivity—to say nothing of "lofty" affirmation.

That there can be no *project* in childbearing is, at the very least, strange. If women are free human beings, why would they not be able to give meaning to their fecundity and answer for being mothers in their own way? Including sometimes refusing maternity. This has not always been either easy or possible, but, throughout time, women have used all means at their disposal to control their fertil-

---

*I have altered the English translation, "the extravagant fecundity of women," to correspond more literally to the original French. *Tr.*

ity. It is because they have now acquired this control that the desire to procreate, in all its intensity, can make its presence felt. After the freedom *not* to conceive, with contraceptive techniques and abortion, women and men now want to exercise, by any means possible, their freedom to conceive. Maternity and paternity are essential human possibilities, and it is often painful to be deprived of them. The opposition between a passively endured destiny and a sovereignly decided project corresponds poorly to the act of giving life, which is simultaneously the effect of both a natural imperative (what was previously called an instinct) and a deliberate project involving a choice.

In this sense, fecundity, realized, is much more than a project. The act of giving life is, to some extent, a natural event, the consequence of the amorous sexual union, but one must also respond to it, give it meaning and value. It is a natural event, because, even if one desires it, provokes it, or helps nature, it is naturally part of the program of the species, the program of life. It is also a call to responsibility, because what "happens" with this event is an existence that is neither physically nor morally self-sufficient, one that must be expressed not in "its supreme truth" but, rather, as the possibility of a meaning. This meaning is never already constituted or immanent, nor is it a matter of a sovereign, solitary decision of an individual; it is sought after in an effort of sharing. It is the effect of the human desire to live with another, to make the other an end and not a means. To give life, for a woman as for a man, cannot be reduced to the fact of enduring, whether you like it or not, the destiny of a species that is doomed to "reproduce itself" and that charges woman with the bulk of this task. You'd have to have no experience of maternity, and no imagination, to reduce childbearing to these, its most biological, aspects. For human beings, bringing a child into the world and raising it from infancy always involves the supreme question of the meaning of existence.

It is because we are conscious, as mortals, that our existence is *finite*, because we know that we are destined to die and to give life, with no semblance of decision in the matter, that the question of responsibility is also so acute. How should we respond to what happens to us, to what happens to humanity in general? The question of birth, which is no less profound than the question of death, is that of thought *seized* by a destiny it has not chosen—living, giving life, dying—and not of a thought that would decide everything itself. It is incomprehensible that thought (like action) might be *seized* by what happens in existence, or that thought itself might have as its task the *seizing* of what happens if immanence and transcendence are brought together.

The freedom to think and act does not consist in negating all necessity, it consists just as much in grasping destiny. Freedom is not necessarily the opposite of destiny. In this sense, it is up to women to *respond* to "biological destiny" itself. Fecundity is a possibility essential to humans (not just women, of course), and gestation, like birth (especially for women), is the advent of a new *situation*, to speak in Sartrean terms. This is why freedom finds a way to fulfil itself here, indeed *more* than elsewhere, under the condition of not being pure negativity.

It is true that freedom can manifest itself as negativity. This concept is found throughout philosophy, from the Cartesian resistance to a deceptive god and the radical doubt that consciousness opposes to this god to the essential possibility of resisting, in which Sartre sees the privileged expression of freedom, and that permits him to write: "we have never been so free as under the Occupation." But freedom contains something else. It should also be thought of as the awareness of necessity. It is in this sense that Spinoza affirmed: "the more I am determined, the more I am free." Indeterminate choices and arbitrary decisions rightly appear to him as the lowest degrees of freedom. Nietzsche was another great thinker regarding necessity: one must recognize, indeed love, necessity. This is what the author of *The Gay Science* calls *amor fati*, love of destiny or love of necessity. We cannot separate the question of women's freedom from the philosophical question of freedom in general and thus from the idea of necessity.

It is no longer forbidden to think that the coming of a child opens a relation to time, the future, and engages us in this temporality confronted by all humans. The coming of a child, even more than many other projects, requires that each person transcend his own small individuality, that he concern himself with the future beyond the duration of his own life. Some would consider, if they happened to lean toward Platonism, that this relation is good for simple people but that elevated minds, more worried about the eternal than the future, have better things to do than bring children into the world. But our time is acutely aware of the fleeting nature of truths as well as civilizations. Temporality seems to affect every thing and every existence. The empty idea of eternity cannot be the basis of our relation to the future, nor can the simple experience of the finitude of things.

The usual way of thinking about time owes still more to the rhythm of life, which brings about the succession of births and deaths and the experience of beginnings and endings, than to the strict opposition of the finite and the infinite. The feeling (*le sentiment*) of time arises, it seems, from the rhythm of nature, the alternation of seasons or days and nights. More than it opposes or compares itself to the eternal (as when Plato says that time is the "mobile image" of eternity), temporality as experience manifests itself in that which differs (*diffère**) and* repeats itself, or repeats itself *in becoming different (se différant***).

Thus human life, beyond the duration of an individual life, seems to maintain itself *in becoming different* from generation to generation. The experience of generation constitutes a fundamental test of difference, one that is connected to sexual difference but that is of another nature. Here, the *human*, both as species and individual (father or mother), has a singular experience of the other: the child is both the same as those who engendered him and an other. He differs, through his singularity, from every woman and every man. This is why every birth is an absolute event.[8] Like sexual difference, the difference of generation prompts us to think about the alterity in identity, the other in the same, and time.

But let us return to the *inequality* of men and women with regard to freedom and action and see how Simone de Beauvoir describes it. While woman is originally burdened with her "biological destiny," man appears "radically different," free and creative: "he nurtures the group, not in the manner of worker bees through a simple vital process, but through acts that transcend his animal nature. *Homo faber* has, from the beginning of time, been an inventor: the stick and the club with which he armed himself to knock down fruits and to slaughter animals became the instruments with which he extends his grasp on the world."[9]

As his stick and his club so clearly prove, man has thus always

---

*The verb *différer* can also have the temporally based, transitive meaning of "to defer" or "postpone." *Tr.*

**Here, the author adds a transitive dimension to the intransitive, or first, meaning of the verb *différer*, "to differ." I have chosen to translate the author's neologistic usage of the reflexive form, *se différer*, as "to become different." *Tr.*

acted by "transcending" his animal condition, while woman, limited to the "natural functions" her biological destiny confines her to, remains mired in their wholly animal immanence. To say that man is "an inventor from the beginning of time" is to consider that he is, *naturally* and *as a man*, free and active, that he is spontaneously led to annex the world and test his power. Woman, to the contrary, is naturally, at least *as woman*, dedicated initially only to her natural functions. As a result, she does not participate in the invaluable inventions of *homo faber*. There would thus be an original rift between the sexes, according to which man is normally and naturally free and active, while woman is by nature destined to maternity, and "thus," passivity.

This point of departure reveals the generally obscured background of the famous diagnosis: "One is not born, but rather becomes, a woman."[10] This judgment means that woman is alienated in her historical condition but implies that she is not born naturally alienated. She *becomes* alienated through the *condition* society has reserved for her. The very term "woman" does not, in this instance, designate a natural sexual identity but a *gender* (*genre*) defined by criteria and constraints specific to a culture.* The woman one "becomes" is, in this instance, that individual deprived of freedom by society. But, if one is not born "woman," in the sense of this alienating and established social femininity, what is a woman, if such a thing exists, *before* becoming a socially inferior and passive being?

Simone de Beauvoir's response is not a simple one. On one hand, women do not exist as natural realities: they are essentially similar

---

*In French, the word for woman, *femme*, means "wife," thus indicating not only sexual identity but also marital status. *Tr.*

to men, just as girls feel similar to boys before their position as object has been imposed upon them. On the other hand, to explain the history of women's alienation, Simone de Beauvoir, in tracing back their acquired condition, considers women, by their very nature, to be suffering from a *handicap*. Their biological destiny initially confines them to this animal state that men, to the contrary, immediately and spontaneously transcend.

This idea of a natural handicap is, in my view, the most debatable of de Beauvoir's themes. It is the very argument that has always been used to explain the subjugation of women: their role in procreation represents a natural inferiority. Again, the classical argument has generally been that women were, in the past at least, unavailable for hunting or war, and from this follows the establishment of a division of roles and tasks. Our philosopher goes even further. She proposes that maternity makes women naturally *passive* and constitutes a natural alienation. The pregnant woman, or even the nursing mother, is "alienated in her body." The child cuts into (*entame*) her physical and moral autonomy as a subject: first as "gratuitous proliferation" in the maternal womb, then as hindrance to the true activities to which a free woman might aspire.

This is why Simone de Beauvoir denounces not one, but two forms of alienation in women, each corresponding to a possible meaning of the word "woman." The first is always cited—expressed by the famous verdict "One is not born, but rather becomes, a woman"—which is a matter of historical, acquired alienation. In this instance, woman is an artificial product. She is made by history, enclosed within a conventional role, obliged to mold herself to the status of an object and to a socially imposed passivity. But, behind this fabricated woman, there is a second, natural woman who is *already alienated*. She is a *biologically trapped* being, above all a victim of her place in a species that destines her to fertility and procreation and thus dooms her to passivity. Women are not simply condemned to passivity by society and according to an arbitrary decree by men. Rather, they are *maintained* in an inertia initially destined by nature. In other words, the fabricated and alienated woman is the woman who remains in her *natural* alienation. In reflecting on this biological destiny she rejects, Simone de Beauvoir might just as well have said: *one does not become woman, one remains woman.*

Maternity did not deserve this brutal denigration—even if it cannot be women's sole mission or constitute an imposed role, and even if the patience and devotion of mothers have long been abused. Certainly, the traditional and flattering praises of the role of mothers, deployed to better separate them from public affairs, has nourished a certain rejection and created a desire to strangle a very self-interested sentimentality. But in denouncing a physical alienation of mothers, remaining blind to what childbearing might have revealed as an original experience of alterity in women, Simone de Beauvoir bears witness to her own ignorance of maternity and, indeed, her disgust for anything related to this experience. Philosophically, this is not the worst of it. Her position also denotes an incapacity to question, even in the slightest, the concept of freedom. Autonomy and self-sufficiency are her only ways of conceiving freedom, putting aside the relation to the other. The trap Simone de Beauvoir is caught in is the point of departure of modern metaphysics—that is, the autonomous subject. This subject always sees in the other either an object or another subject objectivizing him. The other limits me and hinders me, encloses me in his gaze and his projects.

This mode of thought, as I have tried to show elsewhere, can never account for the experience of love, which, for the subject, constitutes a fundamental trial and an experience of sharing. With love, in all its forms, the subject is never autonomous. His freedom is of another order. It is the freedom to transcend his own subjectivity toward the other. Freedom, as I define it, cannot be conceived of as the lofty sovereignty of the subject. It is also the freedom to give, the freedom to accept the demands of the other, and not only the freedom to act upon things or to dominate others. An examination of the motives behind gifts and the gestures they entail would perhaps lead us too far afield, but such an examination would allow us to ascertain the difficulty of defining the gift through categories such as activity and passivity. What does it mean to give oneself? Is it active or passive? What does it mean, for example, to harm oneself for an other? Does a man give himself less in love than a woman? Is the act of giving life active or passive? Are not certain maternal gestures, like that of offering the breast, clearly neither active or passive? All of these behaviors, in fact, inextricably integrate *activity* and *passivity*. This is why it is not as easy, as we seem to think, to classify the sexes according to such categories.

However, the passivity of maternity is even more accentuated in the chapter of *The Second Sex* devoted to the mother. Decidedly, nothing appears to have meaning in childbearing:

> Alienated in her body and in her social dignity, the mother enjoys the comforting illusion of feeling that she is a human being *in herself*, a ready-made *value*. But this is only an illusion. For she does not really make the baby, it makes itself within her; her flesh engenders flesh only, and she is quite incapable of founding an existence that will have to establish itself. . . . The supreme truth of this being creating itself in her belly escapes her. . . . The child in the maternal body is unjustified, it is still only a gratuitous proliferation.[11]

No doubt. . . . It is nevertheless strange to substitute the issue of foundation, which is that of the raison d'être, for that of birth, which is so difficult to fathom. Existentialist philosophy justifiably broke with the old principle of reason, that is, with the idea that in a rational world everything has its reason, exists for a reason. But, if existence is, at its core, without reason, if as Angelus Silesius wrote, "the rose is without why,"[12] if things and beings exist randomly and gratuitously, outside all ultimate finality, it is useless to seek to remedy the absence of foundation through the claim that each being founds itself. It is doubtful that existence can ever "found itself" and finally escape its gratuitousness. Existentialism, like most modern thought, is vain enough to believe in the autonomy of the subject and to recognize therein a privileged form of freedom. To oppose the maternal will to "found" an existence to the necessity that existence found itself is to remain prisoner of a philosophical thinking poorly equipped to theorize birth. This vocabulary is a bit ridiculous: one does not "found" a child. And no one "founds" himself either: each person can, at best, take hold of his destiny. Philosophy has always been uneasy with birth. With few exceptions (such as Kierkegaard), the philosopher sees himself as pure thought—he seems never to have been born. Simone de Beauvoir is still, as philosopher, Plato's granddaughter: she does not mix mind and flesh.

Yet for the mother, her child, and even her unborn child, is immediately something other than an outgrowth of flesh. It is that which she cares for absolutely, that toward which she feels an infinite responsibility. This is why behavior traditionally qualified as "maternal," far from being an enclosure in some sort of immanence can constitute a universal model of an opening to caring (*souci*) *alterity* in general.

The "unjustified" child developing at the maternal breast, from whom might he receive a semblance of justification if it is not from this other who cares for him? This much is well known: if it happens that the child, and then the adult, does not feel completely un-justified, it is because the person who cared for him when he was young counts for something. The psychoanalytic experience, like ordinary experience, teaches this daily. Maternal love, or its substitute, constitutes the fundamental factor in a being's entry into a human world where he can find his place and believe himself justified, despite the gratuitousness of his existence.

Thus, it is surprising to see in the work of a feminist philosopher the reappearance of the metaphysics of Plato's *Banquet*, which reserved for women only the reproduction of bodies and greatly elevated the love of boys under the pretext that this love concerned the fecundation of souls and not of bodies. One day the issues of Western metaphysics's debt to Greek homosexuality and androcentrism's phobia of mixity will have to be addressed.

Masculine humanity always affirms its own power—to know or to be able, to think or to act—and rejects feminine fecundity as the impotence and passivity of materiality and flesh with the same gesture. When Simone de Beauvoir once more describes femininity as originally mired in the flesh, and the mother as the passive instrument of life, she comfirms an ancestral androcentric and metaphysical vision. Completely under the sway of this metaphysical conception, she does not call it into question.

In reality, the identification of the mother with an animal, an essentially carnal, passive being, constitutes an interpretive coup, a very old forceful takeover that women need not support. Nothing justifies maternity being torn from the universe of meaning in this way. Nor that it be opposed to creation and other expressions of freedom. On the contrary, we might expect a woman philosopher to dare to contest the absence of meaning imputed to procreation, not to add to the thinking of childbearing as simple biological destiny; we might expect that instead of adopting the existentialist oppositions of transcendence and immanence, freedom and nature, subject and object, active and passive, to apply them *once again* to the male/female difference, she would have critically questioned these hierarchical conceptual structures.

Is not sexuality precisely the domain in which activity and passivity are the inseparable aspects of the same process? Is it not the domain in which the places of subject and object are interchangeable rather than attributable to two distinct individuals?

These reflections do not in any way imply enclosing women in their carnal fecundity. Naturally women have other ways of being. A woman is not always ready to be a mother, under any condition, at any moment of her life; according to the times, favorable conditions change, as do behaviors. Certain circumstances are necessary for this feminine possibility to be realized and become the expression of a freedom. But, when it is realized, we recognize in desired maternity an uncomparable, singular "passion." A passion that has nothing to do with passivity and from which women, to the contrary, draw a large part of their strength.

Be that as it may, a mother's care for her children, from the moment of gestation, is in complete opposition to a feeling of self-sufficiency or the illusion of being "a value."[13] It is for *the other* that the mother cares, not herself, but, far from seeing this as a sacrifice of self, the responsibility she *takes* for her child is one form of her freedom. This is also true for the child she adopts, or rather, it is the same thing. Maternal responsibility consists in adopting the child that has been conceived. This does not mean that a woman is only a mother, but when she is, she does not mutilate herself, she passionately fulfills a part of herself.

For Simone de Beauvoir and many women after her, the historical emancipation of women required the inverse, that women reject their maternal function to claim the condition of productive, working, active subjects. To be, above all, "like men" was the right way to be free. It was not *with* their femininity but *against* it that women wanted to liberate themselves from historical and natural alienation.

Women today no longer accept this renunciation and this alternative. They want to be free in every possible way, including free to assume their femininity.

Why is creativity never better expressed than through the metaphor of fecundity? Maternity should be reinterpreted as a power and vindicated as a strength. It is a model of creation without being incompatible with all the other forms of creativity or expression through which women might wish to demonstrate their freedom.

THE MASCULINE UNIVERSAL

Women who contest the place made for them in society and claim certain rights "as women" often find themselves accused of "particularism," or "differentialism," while they are only offered, as the sole correct philosophical and republican position, "universalism." This term, which does not, in fact, designate any philosophy, currently evokes a definition of man that must not include any "particular" determination such as religion, language, skin color, or . . . sex. This conception, as we have already stressed, is generally flawed from a logical point of view in that it confuses humanly contingent characteristics, such as color, and humanly universal characteristics such as sex. What is really universal in a logical sense—that is, what involves the totality of a whole—is not being male or being female (obviously one cannot say "all humans are female") but, rather, the fact of being sexed: *all* humans are "either men or women." Taking sexual difference into account, theoretically and practically, does not mean abandoning the universal but, on the contrary, allows us to recognize the concrete and differentiated content of the universal. We could say that each of the sexes is "particular" in the sense that together they give universal humanity all its content. Thus, philosophically, the question is not one of being "for or against" the universal but of giving it its concrete meaning; while abstract universality retains only the most general and formal features of humanity.

To the extent that abstract universalism *neutralizes sexual difference*, it is not compatible with a politics that would seek to transform the relations between the sexes, nor is it compatible with a strategy that would claim to redefine the place of women at the heart of social life. Abstract universalism can, at best, call for equality before the law, which is important but often insufficient, as demonstrated by the real place of women in political life.

This abstract way of thinking is related to a metaphysical tradition opposing, from Plato to Kant and beyond, the world of experience and its contents to that of ideas and abstract forms.

The abstract philosophical point of view considers the individual as a pure thinking subject, independent of his concrete and empirical existence. Thus, he also has no sex. Applied to the realm of law and politics, this abstract vision leads to the consideration of each individual as a neuter subject, independent of any sexual determination. An untenable position in certain domains (family law, labor law, medical ethics, and so on), abstract egalitarianism affirms the *irrelevance* of sexual difference, in the domain of the judicial as well as the political.

Of course, strictly speaking, anything that does not designate a singular existence is, to a certain extent, abstract: to speak of women in general is already to use a category that (like any category) is abstract. The difference between a definition of the essence of man that excludes sex (human being) and one that includes it (man and woman) is thus not simply the distinction between the abstract and the concrete in the sense I have already mentioned. But, if the need to speak and think in terms of general categories forces us into abstraction, the problem is to know *at what level of abstraction* a category is theoretically or practically, and thus politically, operative.

That is why if we say that the concept of humanity or of the sexually *indeterminate* subject is abstract, we mean that these concepts do not permit us to analyze a certain reality correctly or to act upon it.

How are women to name their own experiences, describe their concrete conditions, make their demands heard, if a priori the subject of the law and the citizen must remain sexually indeterminate?

How does one denounce and combat an injustice that hits women in particular (for example, when they are the victims of economic exclusion or inequality) if the category of women is judicially and politically illegitimate? From the moment it is established that there is no difference before the law as to whether one is a man or a woman, women can no longer express themselves *as such* to transform their social status, indeed to defend or promote specific rights. And herein lies the whole problem of knowing if they should speak "as women" or "as human beings."

Because the abstract point of view is a good protector of the status quo and, while today it is constantly repeated that the citizen is *neither man nor woman*, traditional injustices, connected to sexual difference, are reproduced in the spheres of political, social, economic, and family life. The old forms of subordination and exclusion are renewed with no other way of combating them except through continually denouncing the contradiction between the theoretical equality of "human beings" and the inequality in men's and women's conditions, between the equality of laws and de facto inequalities.

However, unless we are to dream of a society where male/female difference would become invisible and insignificant—like that American author who wanted to "abolish gender difference"[1]—we must admit that the two ways of being human will not cease to exist. These two ways of being human generate all sorts of inevitable social and cultural differences—and, moreover, they give rise to inequalities that should be combated. It would be better to say injustices precisely in order to avoid confusing justice with egalitarianism or the strict equalization of conditions. Be that as it may, the problem is not in "abolishing" genders under a supposed indifference of subjects or citizens but in *transforming* the relations between the sexes at the heart of society. *Laboring to make sexual difference play out otherwise*, rather than believing in the possibility of erasing it.

Nevertheless, it is this desire to erase difference that at first tempted feminism. But to efface the difference of "man," meaning human here, has always led to the effacement of woman. According to the principle of the excluded third, abstract universalism always tends to identify the human or the subject with *one of the two terms* of the difference it claims to ignore. Thus, the subject who is "neither man nor woman" is, in the end, conceived according to a masculine model, just as the "man" in the "rights of man" was a citizen of the male sex. And "universalist" feminists have often fallen into the trap of this androcentrism.

In first conceiving of the liberation of women as an equalization of rights and conditions, feminists have actually initiated *a noncritical appropriation of masculine values and models*, accepted without discussion as universal. This is demonstrated, for example, by the acceptance of theories of castration or of maternity as a natural handicap, or with the adoption of Marxist economic and political analyses on the part of many leftist women after World War II.

Inheritors of the old logic of lack, women set themselves the task of repressing what they were lacking (in some sense depriving themselves of their lack), and thus rejoining the human, that is, masculine, universality. Having decided to become human beings "like the others," they were ready to abandon happily all reference to their specificity—including a femininity still to be reinvented— and to renounce their difference, considered an ancestral inferiority. We cannot emphasize enough the delectable logic of the formula, blindly embraced, according to which women wish to be human beings "like the others," since, relative to women, those *others* can only be men. By not questioning themselves about sexual difference, but only about their particularity as women, as if they were the ones who had deviated from the human norm, according to the old androcentric scheme of things, women hoped to get back to generic, or "general," humanity. But no such thing exists, and the erasure of one sex never gives way to neutrality, but to the other sex. We only forget this because we have already situated the masculine and its models in the place of the universal.

Any conception or figuration of the human calls for a masculine or feminine determination. This determination is not a simple empirical variable, like language or hair or skin color. If we can conceive of a human being without taking skin color into account in any way, we cannot think or represent a human being, even schematically, without including the traits that make him or her a man or a woman. There is no asexual human archetype but only two fundamental types—masculine and feminine—with which, moreover, variable characteristics are associated. When we claim not to recognize division, we have already opted for one of the two models and, traditionally, chosen the masculine. The misapprehension of the *two* leading to the affirmation of *one of the two*, the "universalist" logic, has not overcome traditional androcentrism. Rather, it is the modern form of androcentrism.

To retain only one model of humanity is basically what certain feminists desired, in order to reject the difference that had kept them in an inferior and dominated category, to *identify themselves with men*. Androcentrism had no better defender than women when, in their haste to free themselves from their condition, they only imagined assimilating with men and declaring themselves like them, without worrying about rethinking, theoretically or practically, the masculine/feminine opposition or the male-female relationship.

This "virile" feminism would valorize, for example, identification with men in considering a woman who has proved her competency to have shown that she was "like a man." Thus it confirmed that value was essentially masculine and that it was to be found, for the most part, in women who were different, deep down, from their inferior sisters. Paradoxically, sexism was not absent from this form of feminism. It was already apparent through the useful, but severe, critique of certain absurdities, of certain kinds of servility in women who took pleasure in their condition and their passivity. It also seems that liberated women were not averse to being looked upon as exceptions and elevating themselves above other women. There was a benefit, for those who established brilliant careers in the fifties or sixties, in being among those rare women who had risen to important positions. They could feel themselves all the more exceptional, individually, in having come out of the common feminine condition and being ranked with the most recognized men in their fields. They could benefit from the prestige imparted by "masculine" qualities (precisely as an exception) and, at the same time, the considerations traditionally due to women (as women). No doubt they were not reluctant to think of themselves as beings of a third sort, basically not very concerned with revolutionizing the social order—from the moment it permitted their own advancement—and not always regarding the ascension of their feminine companions favorably.

The mass promotion of women in society in some sense made the success of these women pioneers seem commonplace, and still today we can truly sense, in the resistance to the implementation of conditions favorable to this promotion, a nostalgia on the part of certain women for their status as *exception*.

If the masculine model and values have dominated political and philosophical thought, the adoption of these models has also compromised the critique of the economic exploitation of women that lies at the heart of the family structure. Winning political and civil rights and struggling to gain access to all professions has somewhat overshadowed the critique of this economic exclusion.

Economic exclusion must not be taken to mean simply that women—at least those of the middle class (lower, middle, and upper)—have been kept in the home, financially dependent on either their own families or their husbands. Inversely, we must also take into account *the exclusion of domestic feminine labor* from the economic sphere.

As a modern consequence of the sexual division of labor, the private familial space, left to the responsibility of women, has remained outside the economic space proper. The work done there does not exist as recognized labor. If the need for women to earn a living "outside" to achieve economic freedom has been brought to the fore, and rightly so, the unpaid nature of labor "inside" the home has not been properly addressed, as if the exclusion of the home from the modern economy went without saying.

In fact, this problem was posed from the first international feminist congress in 1878[2] when women asked for the recognition of housework as labor in its own right. In the same spirit, at the tenth major feminist congress, women called for a right to retirement for "the housewife who has raised one or more children" and "who has always done everything in her home."[3] But these demands never succeeded, although, like a sea serpent, the question of housework periodically returns, without ever finding a viable solution.

In fact, the economic system has ignored feminine labor inside the home in order not to encroach upon the private sphere, the reserved site of patriarchal power. This domestic exploitation is well known. It has often been denounced, but the means of combating it have not yet been provided.

The only way of thinking about economic freedom consisted in having women enter into the economic sphere (capitalist or socialist) as it was. The idea was that putting an end to the domestic exploitation of women meant women had to leave the home. No doubt this was right. But, in doing this, the private space was maintained as such, while it might have been transformed through, for example, integration into the global economic space. But that would have required calling into question the opposition between the two spheres, public and private, and giving domestic labor a price tag. Instead, the stupidity of domestic labor was denounced.

We must ask ourselves why the depreciation of the labor (and the status) of housewives was so easily accepted, why the exploitation involved was not criticized. It is a little as if, instead of denouncing the exploitation of the labor of the working class, it had been argued that this labor was stupid and contemptible and that the workers should leave the factory and completely change their activity.

The fundamental role of women in the home was so undervalued that no one has tried to find the means for replacing them. It is moreover politically incorrect, above all on the left, to ask questions about this subject since it is understood that it is degrading to waste time bothering with household tasks and, indeed, with children. However, is housework, no matter what certain feminists say (those for whom housework is necessarily shameful and contemptible), any less respectable or useful than many other kinds of labor remunerated on the market? Housework implies a great diversity of tasks compared to those required by other kinds of employment. In fact, the intrinsic value of this labor, indeed its interest, has been denied due to its lack of market value.

Simone de Beauvoir does not have words harsh enough to describe the emptiness and the absurdity of tasks related to the maintenance of the household, tasks incapable of giving women the opportunity for a "singular affirmation of themselves." But does any labor exercised *outside* the home necessarily permit, *for women as for men*, a singular affirmation of oneself? What an idealization of labor! What a myth of "exteriority"! In reality, what is in question is not the "interior" but, rather, its place in the symbolic and economic order. It is true that, for Simone de Beauvoir, any concern with *the interior*, including the concern for décor and ornamentation, is completely useless; it merely bears witness to a lack of true interiority, to the incapacity for authentic contemplation. Those who create their own world, like artists, do not care about their "interiors": "Among others, artists, who have been given the task of recreating the world through matter—sculptors and painters—are altogether oblivious as to the environment in which they live."[4]

This remark, neither true nor false (can one generalize in this way?), is quite disconcerting because, as often happens, de Beauvoir does not seem to recognize any intermediary between, on the one hand, the creative genius who "transcends himself" in his works or realizes himself in his acts and, on the other, the poor sado-masochistic housewife who pathetically attempts to fix up her home as best she can and "transform her prison into a palace."

What is intolerable in the housewife's role and work is not at all the nature of these tasks but, rather, the fact that they are accomplished without pay and excluded from labor considered to be "productive."

In reality, women have acquired their independence and their dignity by working *outside* the home—that is, by exercising a re-munerated activity—but they have not transformed the traditional division of tasks and responsibilities at the heart of domestic life. Thus what has rightly been called the *double work day* has become the rule for most women of modest or average means (others unload most of the housework on household workers). The first feminism thought that women's advancement to men's statuses and places would be enough to set them free, but in fact this liberation only touched, at best, a part of the privileged middle class. For the most part women conserved their traditional roles, or else accumulated tasks, or only enjoyed their freedom by remaining single and renouncing family.

The relegation of feminine labor to the private sphere was accompanied by a certain lack of interest in this question on the part of the most privileged and cultivated, those least confronted with this problem and who, as a result of their studies and their professions, effectively scorned housework. These women had no other models than that of middle-class and masculine success.

In exclusively privileging the masculine model of activity, however, they forgot to ask how, in exercising a profession, indeed, in ambitiously developing a career, women could actually live like men, since the majority of men had wives at home to prepare dinner in the evening and take care of the housework and the children during the day. But most women didn't have a "woman at home"— a total dissymetry experienced by all working women—even the most well-off.

One obvious solution to this problem was to share domestic tasks, so that women would labor like men and men, likewise, would begin to work like women and consequently share the cleaning, cooking, and child-rearing. Why hasn't this family equality, this symmetry in roles, been possible? Why does it still function so poorly? Women's responsibility for material life continues, in fact, practically unchanged, still today, in most couples and families. The lack of shared domestic tasks and responsibilities is feminism's most bitter failure. Doubtless because it has met with fierce resistance on the part of men, but also because, in this domain, it was hoped that everything would change through mindset and good will, and nothing was expected of the law. The family economy remained a private terrain, closed to any possible reform and the chosen site for the reproduction of habits. Women resigned themselves to take on the essential household responsibilities, whether they worked or not, and under more or less difficult conditions.

Shouldn't the exploitation of housewives have been combated much more vigorously, and the invaluable cultural and economic value of their actions and their labor recognized? It's a difficult question. For this to have happened, it would have been necessary to recognize the economic place of their tasks, give them a price, and thus provoke the entrance of domestic labor into the general system of exchange. This undertaking would have required a profound calling into question of the entire economic system and the creation of original solutions—both inside and outside (reduction of work time for men and women, childcare development, indeed, remuneration for domestic labor no matter who is doing it). Such an approach would have seemed conservative, and it would have been suspected, as we well know, of seeking to "keep women in the home." But many women had no choice and, in reality, did remain in the home. Domestic exploitation has thus continued as such, above all among the lower-middle and working classes.

It is, however, a complete contradiction to maintain that, when carried out by a man or a woman employed in the home, domestic labor must be remunerated like any other service, and yet, when carried out by a woman within the family framework, this labor is no longer worth anything. It is considered normal to pay for the services of professional cleaners, cooks, waiters and waitresses, carpet cleaners, to say nothing of daycare workers. But the mother of the family should do all this without pay.

In reality, the unpaid nature of family household labor and its a priori exclusion from the modern economic system constitute an original and virtually hidden form of exploitation. This is all the more so since in our culture the private sphere and the (economic and political) modern public sphere remain foreign to each other. In the ancient Greek world women were confined to the space of the home and did not have access to public life, but the home (*oïkos*) was the principal space of production and gave the economy its name (the means of managing the business of the *oïkos*, of the home). In contemporary times, in our culture, the domestic space is a place of exclusion: the "housewife," even if she works all day to maintain the family's daily life, *does not exist* "economically." It is thus understandable that women have put all their energy into getting out of the home and earning a living in order to acquire a social existence and become independent. But this move should have been accompanied by a radical critique of the economy. It should have been necessary to call into question a system that gives women heavy domestic responsibilities while at the same time permitting the complacent affirmation that women at home *do not labor.*

Since the nineteen-fifties women have preferred to work *outside* and then solve the problem of the home. Certainly anything was better than remaining in that condition of a natural domestic, stripped of any social recognition, of any status, of any revenue (since the financial difficulties of modest couples often obliged women to contribute a "second salary"). Women of the cultivated bourgeoisie, or those who had gotten through their studies, could strive to practice a worthwhile profession and "get help" in the home. They admitted that caring for the home and children represented real labor and justified a salary—if this labor was assumed by employees. As for women in modest and working-class milieus, far more alienated than others, either they had no choice and little consciousness of their condition or, in solidarity with their circles, they were, above all, sensitive to class conflicts. Marxists claimed to be conscious of the particular form of the exploitation of women: Engels had even written that in the family the husband was the bourgeois and the wife the proletarian. . . . But they believed that only revolution could put an end to the alienation of both women and the proletariat. For August Bebel,[5] the most feminist of socialists, it is communal life and the erasure of the old private sphere that must liberate women.

The development of "domestic science," as it was called in the nineteen-fifties, helped to lesson the problem by objectively diminishing the amount of domestic labor necessary, as well as its duration. It is certain that, without the proliferation of innovations in the form of household and hygienic appliances, women would not have continued to assume domestic tasks alone, as they have generally done. They would have required that certain necessities of daily life, such as the laundry and the cooking, be relegated to the outside, just as they have had recourse to daycare centers for their young children.

A phenomenon of *exteriorization* of traditionally domestic services has, moreover, occurred all the same. Not through abandoning the private sphere in favor of communal life but through industrializing and commercializing numerous services. The portion of things made in the home has diminished extraordinarily, especially in the area of food, but everything made outside is expensive and penalizes women from the most modest circles. It is above all these women who assume the double work day.

But what is most important remains the education of children, one of humanity's most noble and necessary tasks. There again, the attempt to denigrate those essential functions was unrelenting, because they were carried out by women within the private space, in that no man's land, whereas their economic and cultural necessity should have been acknowledged.

The care of children, however, has helped to keep women at home. Is this responsibility as artificial and imposed as some would like to think? It will be up to women to answer freely that question the day they are no longer ashamed to claim their desire in this domain. When they have the means and the strength to have these values—scorned by an essentially masculine ideology—recognized and, indeed, shared. Is there proof that women in general dream only of unloading the care of their children onto others? I fear that old models of liberation have, on these questions as well, blinded us a little and nourished a contempt for women's traditional role.

It was difficult, however, to proceed otherwise. It couldn't have been a question of confining women to the traditional "housewife" role that closed off their access to the common space: thus the margin to maneuver was very tight. But was it necessary, for all that, to stake everything on the *outside* and on masculine models without asking how the new relationship between inside and outside was to be treated? Perhaps it was necessary to change domestic life as well as ways of working outside in order to make economic life compatible with private life and to reconcile the domestic economy with the global economic system.

The question of the sexual division of labor in private life has not yet been resolved. And society must provide a means of replacing women as well as a domestic structure capable of childcare and education. Society is very far from doing this today. Children in the most modest circumstances suffer most from this deficiency.

Whatever the economic evolution of society, it is essential that the family economy wherein woman is the natural servant disappear and that all labor enter into the general economic system. This supposes a transformation of the opposition of *inside* and *outside*—that is, a change in ways of working in general, on the inside as on the outside, notably through diminishing the duration of labor for men as for women.

Already, taking into account new techniques and the use of machines, we can anticipate that the quantity of human labor necessary for production will continue to decrease. On one hand, because of unemployment, remunerated labor—more and more rare—is all the more valorized. On the other, as a result of technological progress, notably in manual labor, the old form of productive labor is becoming devalued. Everyone suspects that the question, tomorrow, will be to know how millions of people whose labor is no longer necessary to production will live. It will of course be necessary to distribute wealth otherwise, but also to live differently. Private life and the domestic domain will be looked at in a new way.

After 1968 androcentric feminism gave way to a new feminism, which often rejected this label and tried to break with masculine models. Even though a certain number of studies continued along the path forged by Simone de Beauvoir,[6] women's specificity became the privileged object of feminist research, and masculine values were replaced by feminine ones. This betrayal of "universalism" was needed to escape the androcentric trap, but it fell into another trap that might be called "separatist" and "communitarian." American women called this trend "radical feminism."

One strove to think of femininity separately, beginning with femininity itself and exalting, sometimes quite narcissistically, the body and feminine desires. Independent of the masculine gaze or masculine desire, women abandoned themselves to themselves and each other with delight and pride reclaiming their own self-sufficiency. I continue to think that this extreme moment was beautiful, interesting, and necessary because women entered into a new relation with each other. A novel form of solidarity and friendship was born in this period. This movement inspired diverse and original literary and theoretical works, such as those of Hélène Cixous, Catherine Clément, and Luce Irigaray.

But it was difficult to remain in this splendid isolation. Except for those who permanently associated masculine domination with the constraints of relations between the two sexes, and for whom the choice of homosexuality appeared as the only way of ending their alienation.

This position, in its most radical formulation, contested the very necessity of defining the sexes. If sexual identity only takes on meaning within heterosexual relations, which oppress women, the very categories of men and women must be erased, especially in the eyes of those women who were breaking off all private relations with men. The idea was that, far from expressing a natural reality, sexual difference in fact designated a class difference expressed in the difference between names: *men* and *women*, oppressors and oppressed. In other words, "heterosexual culture" was the cause of women's oppression and the basis of sexual "classes." As certain American movements maintained at this time,[7] the homosexual choice was becoming a political choice and the only way for women to win their independence was to opt for "the lesbian way of life." Pushed to the limit, as Monique Wittig wrote, "lesbians are not women." "Lesbians absolutely do not ask themselves the question of knowing what a woman is: it would be improper to say that lesbians live, associate, and make love with women, because "woman" only makes sense in heterosexual systems of thought and heterosexual economic systems."[8] In its radicality, this position expresses a part of the truth, which is that the sexes really do take on meaning and value through their difference and interrelations. To this extent, perhaps the homosexual choice constitutes a sort of effacement of *sexual* identity in the traditional sense of the term.

In their respective radicality, separatism and universalism can thus each lead to forms of an eclipsing of mixity: separatism in exalting difference to the point of dreaming of a separation of the sexes—indeed, a homosexual culture; universalism in denying the difference of the sexes or disguising the privilege of the masculine model under the so-called sexual neutrality of subjects.

It would be better to pose the question differently, to begin again from *two* and not from the *one*. Because multiplicity and diversity necessarily derive from this original difference. It no longer suffices to reflect upon the identities and freedoms of women; we must rethink the meaning of a truly mixed society in which everyone, men and women, must feel responsible.

That is why women are now breaking from universalist apoliticism as well as the separatist retreat and recognizing the sexual dimension of politics and the political dimension of the relation between the sexes.

A modern "feminism" should no longer be a theory or a politics of women but, rather, it should be grounded in a philosophy of mixity. In other words, *thought on mixity will be postfeminist*. It must abandon masculine models as well as purely feminine ones when they are considered unilaterally, while at the same time inscribing women's outlook and presence in society.

The universalist temptation was to neutralize sexual difference to the benefit of the universality of the subject. Today, it is a matter of the inverse, of *politicizing sexual difference*—that is, working to constantly reinvent the meaning of this difference.

To think about mixity is to consider that there are two versions of the human (*l'homme*) and to represent humanity as a couple. Politicizing difference involves a political translation of the value of mixity.

Filiations

IDENTITY AND HOMOSEXUALITY

The masculine and the feminine, which can just as easily designate natural sexual characteristics as symbolic distinctions, are not sufficient for defining sexual identity—assuming one should do this—or, therefore, for defining individuals as men or women. Depending upon the society in question, these categories take on more or less extensive meanings and practical consequences.

One is born a boy or girl, but how does one become a *man* or a *woman*?

Most often, in traditional societies, it is through matrimonial status and the fact of having children. Men and women are not only defined by innate characteristics but also by the fact that they can be, or are, fathers or mothers. This principle surprises us today, but even in contemporary Western societies, the fact of having or not having children plays an important role in the feeling of belonging to a sex. There is a sort of "sex consciousness," just as we speak of "class consciousness," which accompanies the experience of procreation, even more so than the experience of "sexuality." But perhaps there is something specifically feminine here? Sometimes I have this suspicion: What if sexual difference, instead of going back to the difference between two things of the same order, led us to discover that man and woman are not speaking of the same thing when they speak of the sexes? If the masculine and the feminine were not only the double form of the human but, beyond the symmetries and the dissymmetries, and under the unifying category of sex, it were a question of two profoundly different human realities that, in the end, might be without exact equivalent? And moreover, isn't it only in this way that there can be two sexes, and not just variations of one? Perhaps maternity is what reveals a feminine specificity with no masculine equivalent. A full recognition of the heterogeneity of the species is dizzying.

We might wonder, coming back to models of traditional societies, if sexual identity cannot remain vague, or with little social significance, as long as the individual does not enter into a matrimonial relationship and has no descendants. Thus, Claude Lévi-Strauss emphasizes "the true sense of repulsion most societies experience with regard to the unmarried." He notes that almost all societies "place the matrimonial status at a very high level" and classify "men" not only according to their natural sex or age but also according to their status as unmarried, or as married without children, or finally as a fathers of families. It is only with the birth of the first child that a man becomes an adult and enjoys all of the rights of adulthood. In extreme cases, as with the Bororo, the conditions of material existence are so closely linked to marriage that an unmarried person "is really only half a human being"![1] Fortunately, modern societies have valorized the individual and his freedom and promoted the unmarried man or woman to the status of full human being. These traditional familial and social structures seem archaic today. And it has been established, in principle if not always in fact, that the individual can, and even should, be self-sufficient, if he does not want to fall back into dependency on another man or woman. This is the point upon which Simone de Beauvoir rightly insists.

However, as astonishing as the individual's outdated economic dependency upon the other sex may seem to us, this is also exactly what Aristotle was already thinking about when he said that man and woman were "two beings incapable of existing without each other."[2]

There are other reasons why man and woman "cannot exist without each other"—other dependencies: erotic dependence, for pleasure; biological dependence, for procreation; and emotional dependence, which involves all the others. As I have previously attempted to show, the desire to procreate is not *only* of a biological order but necessarily implies a biological dependence. However, in affirming, with Aristotle, that man and woman cannot exist without each other, we place ourselves in the general position of an interdependence of the two sexes.

I will be criticized, no doubt, for considering this mutual dependence *natural* here and thus implicitly admitting that humanity is *naturally* heterosexual. I adopt this starting point as a matter of evidence. Humans, universally sexed, are *generally* animated by desire for the other and depend on this other to procreate—which they also desire, *in general*. Exclusive interest in the same sex is accidental, a sort of exception—even a frequent one—that confirms the rule. This formulation is based on classical Aristotelian distinctions: what is *necessary* is without exception (it is said to be *always* the case, like a mathematical theorem); what is *general* usually occurs but admits exceptions (it is said to be *most often* the case, like a product of nature); finally, what is *accidental* occurs *sometimes.*

How to think about sexual difference when the sexes cease to depend upon each other, when they split apart, and when, instead of desire for the other sex, we encounter desire for the same—what, today, we call *homosexuality*? I should put this word in quotation marks, because like heterosexuality, this recent category poses many questions. But these two words are now so commonly used that this precaution would seem a bit artificial.

The first question here would be to know if the choice of amorous objects, "homosexual" or "heterosexual," affects, and in what sense, sexual difference, and if it must contribute to the definition of an individual's *"sexual" identity*. Must each person socially define himself as *"homo"* or *"hetero,"* and what is this identity that relates to sex in a new way?

The very possibility of asking these questions stems from the fact that the notion of *sexuality* seems to have been completely displaced. As a rule, it used to involve sexual difference as it related to generation. Biological sexuality corresponded to a social "sexuality" expressed through institutions such as marriage and filiation. It was believed that the masculine/feminine distinction could be superimposed onto the distinctions of husband/wife or mother/father. Sexual difference—and thus also the *effects of identities* it produced—was essentially linked to the different roles played in generation, the object of so many interpretations. This basis for difference seems essential to Françoise Héritier who doesn't locate sexual difference—and its stakes—at the level of anatomical sex but, rather, at the level of generation, and thus at the level of women's fecundity.

However, love is not only defined by its fecundity. This term also applies to erotic relations, independent of any progeny; and, parodying Plato, we might distinguish between two goddesses of love, or two goddesses of sex: Aphrodite the Fecund and Aphrodite the Voluptuous—one a goddess of life, and the other a goddess of eroticism. Fortunately, these goddesses are sisters and can associate.

About our second Aphrodite, the voluptuous one, we will nonetheless say that she seems less strictly linked to sexual difference than her sister, the fecund one. Because there is no essential reason why pleasure could not leave sexual difference a little vague. Voluptuousness can do without this difference.

But, in the erotic relations between two people of the same sex, the goddess of pleasure never meets the one of fecundity. That is her law.

The structure of masculine homosexual desire, as it is portrayed in certain literary accounts, allows for yet another division, not widespread but frequently seen, the division between sex and love: on one hand, the pleasure of *pure sex*, that is, eroticism, and, on the other, the pure pleasure of the *absence of sex*. Thus everything happens as if body and soul, or flesh and spirit, should not mix but, rather, coexist separately.

These forms are perhaps two aspects of the same desire for purity: on one side, nothing but *sex* and only *one* sex, without mixture, without mixity; on the other, nothing sexual, no sex at all, only love of the soul, without the impurity of mixing with the body.

We might point out to what extent authors such as André Gide, Colette, Julien Green, or Mishima have illustrated this double desire for purity: the simultaneous pleasure of sex, unmixed, a homosexual desire ardently enamored of bodies, and a metaphysical and mystical taste for purity without body. Speaking of Gide,

Genet, and Mishima, Catherine Millot writes: "What constitutes their shared horror is mixture, the impure. . . . they are Cathares who want good and evil at the same time, in all its purity: the disembodied spirit, the mute flesh, desire without love, each term brought to its perfection of being unmixed. What they reject is Incarnation, the Word made flesh." The complicity between metaphysics and homosexual anguish over mixing is expressed this way in *Confession d'un masque*: "There existed in me a pure and simple division between spirit and flesh." It seems that in homosexual desire, at least in this frequent masculine type, there is a fetishistic worship of the male organ, apart from its generative function. Genet attests to this when he recognizes that rejecting mixity, the mixing of the sexes, has something to do with rejecting procreation.

In their own way, all of these authors replay the old Platonic division between body and soul. But only to a certain extent, because if Plato, in *The Banquet*, opposes men's love for women to their love for boys, the latter addresses their souls, not their bodies. In this dialogue, Aphrodite the Popular continues to incarnate fecund love, love that seeks eternity through the fecundation of women's bodies, while Aphrodite the Celestial incarnates the love of eternal truths through the "fecundation of souls" alone—souls of boys, not girls.

The love of women is good for those who wish to survive through their children (common desire), while the sublimated love of boys is good for those who want to contemplate eternal ideas. *Sublimated* love, no doubt, since Socrates rejects the advances of Alcibiades. But, and here is the affinity between the writers just mentioned, impurity is altogether on the side of the feminine body and procreation, while the beauty of boys is more pure, and still more pure is the beauty of ideas.

Might we still be Platonists? One of the traits of our age is that sexual life is increasingly defined by pleasure, while procreation is only occasionally associated with sexuality—when it is not clearly dissociated. Thanks also in part to certain aspects of the Freudian approach (though not all of them), we have come to conceive of sexual life as independent from procreation. That is why, despite the privilege Freud continued to accord to "genital" sexuality, we are increasingly interested in diverse forms of sexual pleasure, in desire and its "objects." Anything love is directed toward becomes the libido's *object*. At the beginning of the twentieth century, we begin to speak of homosexuality in order to define the sexuality of those for whom the preferred "love object" is a person of the same sex (from the Greek *homo*, the same) and not a person of the *other* sex (*hetero*). From classifying objects (of pleasure or of love), we move to classifying subjects, and we divide the *subjects* of desire into two categories: *homosexuals* and *heterosexuals*.

This new nomenclature offers the advantage of holding to a sort of description of desire, without value judgment and, through the symmetrical construction of the two words, of creating an equality of the two types of sexual "object choice."

But, for the same reasons, this nomenclature presents certain drawbacks. Because, if Freud no longer excludes those formerly called "inverts," whether this exclusion stems from common morality or psychiatry (which considered homosexuality as a kind of mental illness), he does not go so far as to consider sexuality outside all "norms." Without passing any judgment on the total personality, homosexuality, for the father of psychoanalysis, basically remains a kind of exception in relation to the "normal" development of the libido, even if this "normalcy" itself is based much more on the demands of civilization than on nature.

Above all, Freud brings to light the bisexual disposition of every subject, which means that the "object choice" onto which the libido will fix is the result of a complicated and uncertain venture. Thus the Oedipal complex, its outcome so decisive for subsequent sex life, is already double itself, and Freud describes its two forms as positive and negative (or inverted). So it seems that homosexuality, rather than being in absolute contradiction with nature, represents one human possibility. However, a synthesis follows the infantile bisexual dispositions and partial drives, a synthesis that, in principle, links access to sexual identity and the fixation of the libido on a type of object that—most often—is of a sex other than that of the subject. Civilization's interests, to a certain extent, meet up with those of biological and psychic life and contribute to the repression of one of the two possibilities offered by the initial bisexuality. These two possibilities are not altogether equivalent. If Freud terms as "inverted" the Oedipal form that, duplicating the other, places the boy in an amorous and feminine position vis-à-vis the father, it is because the "positive" form conforms to the status of boyhood. Freud expresses this by saying that, according to this inverted form that reduplicates the other, "the boy behaves simultaneously as a girl."[4] Thus, the "positive" form of the complex is supported by the biological sex of the child. Furthermore, if the Oedipus complex is double, it is because, beyond these initial "dispositions," each child is born of a parental couple that is mixed in both the real and the symbolic. Through its contradictions and from its onset, this structure programs the need for the child to choose an identity for himself and to choose objects, which are themselves sexed.

Thus Freud demonstrates that the sexual dichotomy poses different problems for every "subject": the problem of access to a masculine or feminine sexual identity, and that of structuring desire and object choices. If these two problems are linked, they are not, strictly speaking, identical.

Defining oneself as male or female (*masculin ou féminin*) involves the sexual identity of the subject, while homosexuality remains a question of the "object choice," of the structuration of desire. From a psychoanalytic point of view, the homosexual choice, despite the problems it raises, does not call into question either sexual difference or the ultimate anchoring of this difference in generation. Conversely, since the mid-nineteen-seventies in the United States, *gay studies* and *lesbian studies* have often tried to prove that genders are the result of a cultural construction, thus, at the same time, greatly relativizing the difference between "homosexuality" and "heterosexuality."

Whatever the case may be, perhaps we have not been attentive enough to this slippage in meaning that has moved from classifying *objects* of desire to classifying *subjects* in general, and that now raises questions concerning individual, and even community identity. One of the consequences of this slippage has been the construction of a new sexual classification of individuals involving neither their sex nor their gender but, rather, their tastes,* enclosing each individual in a definitive, fixed determination.

The new dichotomy between homosexuality and heterosexuality poses boundary problems as complicated as those of sexual division. Through its symmetry in terms, it profoundly transforms the status of "excentric" forms of love or desire. More and more, homosexuality is considered one form of sexuality, equivalent to the general form, and not as an exception to or transgression of the general law. For some, it has become the defining characteristic of a "minority

---

*We now speak, in France, of "sexual orientation." *Author's note to the English translation.*

culture" facing a more or less oppressive heterosexual "majority." At least this is the "politically correct" view of homosexuality.

Thus homosexuality becomes a new trait in determining identity, and the homosexual/heterosexual opposition almost tends to replace the masculine/feminine one. Likewise, homosexual politics are developing and involve different choices and strategies. These theories and politics are urgent and legitimate in their own right. They raise questions of another order than those we have posed here.

Contrary to parallels so often drawn by certain trends in feminism, in France as well as in the United States, the cause of women in general is different from that of male and female homosexuals, simply because women cannot define themselves as a minority. What's more, the concept of homosexuality comes to mask the profound difference separating the sexuality of women among themselves and that of men among themselves. So much so that it contributes to the perception that the interests of gays and lesbians are necessarily the same. This may not be the case. We might also wonder if the category "homosexuality" doesn't serve as a screen for less simplistic approaches to sexual life.

To the extent that we can speak of "homosexual politics"— expressed especially through movements and positions—we may note that there are *several possible politics*. One privileges the singularity of individual, private choice, and demands respect but does not claim to construct a more generally applicable model. And one seeks to develop a model for life in general, specific to one minority group, indeed equivalent to the general heterosexual model. Within the framework of this second politics, certain individuals call for rights strictly identical to those of "heterosexuals," including those concerning marriage and procreation. (There we have a double general orientation that does not claim to cover all existing positions.)

Corresponding to these two orientations are two strategies, each of them political and each concerning the place and rights of homosexuals within the city-state. The first involves an *uncompromising struggle for the sexual freedom* of both sexes and thus for an absolute respect for private life—as long as no crimes are involved. It presupposes a consistent policy of tolerance with regard to sexual orientation and takes a stand against any segregation based on personal values. It can contain a certain valorization of deviance, even of transgression, and it defends the right to singularity more than the desire for assimilation into the general order. (This position might, moreover, be accompanied by a new status for single men and women whom our societies continue to bully more or less openly.) The single person, even more so than communal living, represents an eternally subversive lifestyle, because it is a lifestyle that maintains the separate and secret nature of private life.

Such a strategy of tolerance has the advantage of being universally applicable. Each individual can stake certain claims, regardless of his sexual classification. It returns all the pleasures of love or sex to the private sphere, including that of heterosexuals (who aren't necessarily married).

The second strategy would lead, rather, to *the construction of new lifestyles*, the development of another culture, and the recognition, within traditional society, of the existence of *new communities* affirming different values and behaviors. This trend, American in origin, also imposes its vocabulary, and one now speaks of gay culture. It is inscribed in the post-1968 liberation movements, which valorized the invention of new lifestyles.

I'm not sure if the model of the "homosexual couple" falls within the latter trend. On one hand, it really does constitute a new way of living and embracing homosexuality. On the other, it represents an official expression of homosexuality modeled on the heterosexual paradigm and on the figure of the mixed couple. This figure may have a strategic function, since it allows homosexual couples to claim the same rights as heterosexuals, including rights concerning procreation.

However, if the homosexual couple is increasingly recognized in contemporary society, and we should applaud this, we might wonder whether the homosexual couple can be equated with the mixed couple as a parental couple. We are speaking here, of course, of the case in which two people of the same sex, with recourse to medically assisted procreation, would claim legal parental rights over a child who would thereby be recognized as the son or daughter of two men or two women. We are not speaking here of particular cases whose circumstances might lead two men or two women, or more, whatever the nature of their relationship, to *raise* a child together. These cases are always possible and often desirable if circumstances have deprived a child of his parents. This does not pose a problem in principal if the origin or the filiation of the child is not at stake. The question is one of rights, and thus of norms and institutions, not of de facto situations.

While not unanimously accepted, the choice of a "politics of the couple" has gradually taken hold because it offers *the advantage and the inconvenience* of describing the homosexual relationship as the replication, between people of the same sex, of the "heterosexual" couple.

An advantage, because, by calling for equal rights for all kinds of couples ("homo" or "hetero"), the possibility of instituting legal relations between men and women who live together, such as the PACS,* was created. The importance of such a possibility is obvi-

---

*The *"Pacte civil de solidarité"* (the Civil Pact of Solidarity), created in 1999, gives numerous rights to couples, homosexual or otherwise, without being tanous, and the distress brought on by the AIDS epidemic alone justifies the creation of this new type of contract. This choice also allows for the social recognition of a lifestyle and lends it legitimacy. In addition, this model fundamentally reassures the "right-thinking" who find therein a familiar psychological, emotional, and social structure.

But the inconvenience of such a model, which certain people question, is the somewhat "fabricated" character of this couple that, in imitating the mixed couple, hides the singular nature of lifestyles and the diverse forms of desire behind this structure. It claims, moreover, to apply equally to the two sexes, while the erotic or amorous relationships between women are not the same as those between men. Just as there is no sameness or symmetry between the sexual behaviors of man and woman, there is no symmetry between what we would like to describe simply as *two "homosexualities."*

If this conjugal model is not claimed by all gays, it is especially because it does not correspond to the way men experience their sexuality.

The cinema often offers edifying representations of the "homosexual couple," as if presenting to the general public a sentimental and sterilized image of a sexual lifestyle—for example, the American film *Philadelphia*—conclusively silences its originality or transgressive aspects. On the other hand, a film such as *Cruising* by Bruce LaBruce and Rick Castro crudely shows the hot spots of the gay scene on Santa Monica Boulevard, West Hollywood, with its prostitution, its fetishistic and sadomasochistic practices, its collective

---

tamount to marriage. But for single people adoption is possible at the individual level. *Author's note to the English translation.*

and violent forms of satisfaction. These images, in contrast to many others, do not seek to portray particular sexual practices as either banal or normal. To the contrary, Rick Castro absolutely refuses to tack models of "hetero-"sexuality onto gays. He declares in an interview: "Certain people in the gay community try to transpose hetero values of sex and love onto homosexuals, and they say: 'We are the same. We fall in love and have sexual relations just like everyone else.' But I believe that this is not at all true. . . . Many gay men are looking for the perfect man. They have *very specific criteria* as to what turns them on sexually."[5] With this reference to precise criteria conditioning desire, Rick Castro reclaims the "perverse" structuration (in the psychoanalytic sense of the term) of male homosexual desires. The multiplicity of sexual partners plays an essential role here because the taste for a specific criterion counts more than the choice of a person. Bruce LaBruce emphasizes that in his opinion, "homosexuality is very morbid" and that it has "a dark side."

It would be naïve to attribute the "dark" side of sexuality, or to generalize this perverse dimension of desire, to masculine homosexuality alone. But why even want to identify particular forms of desire with traditional structures that are so very different?

Even Michel Foucault, hardly someone suspected of wanting to trivialize forms of desire, is drawn to use both provocative and reassuring images of homosexuality. The ordinary representation of masculine homosexuality, he explains, is "two guys meeting in the street, seducing each other with a glance, putting their hands on each other's asses, and getting it on in fifteen minutes."[6] This representation is not completely incorrect for Foucault, but he finds it superficial and rather reassuring. According to him, it is a "tidy image of homosexuality" that disturbs no one. Perhaps. What is troubling about homosexuality, for Foucault, is not the imagining of "a sexual act not in conformity with the law or nature; that's not what disturbs people. But that individuals begin to love each other, that's the problem." No doubt, this reversal of perspective is astute, but it rings untrue. Public opinion always reconciles with homosexuality as soon as love and friendship are mentioned. It is moved; it approves. What disturbs the public is, despite what Foucault says, the transgression of the law, sodomy, and the multiplication of partners. Is this reason enough to want to erase unusual forms of sexuality, or is it better to assume them as different forms, outside the common norms. There is a choice to be made here. All the more so since society's intolerance and incredible violence toward homosexuals, all too prevalent until not so long ago, have disappeared. Previously, transgression was identified with crime. This is no longer the case. But just because transgression is not a crime doesn't mean that it should become a norm.

For many homosexuals there is a contradiction, an irresolvable one perhaps, between the desire to proudly assume an "eccentric" and transgressive position—this is the temptation of any sexual freedom sovereignly affirmed—and, at the same time, the fear of exclusion, the desire for integration, even the nostalgia for a normal family life. Gay Pride expresses this contradiction, combining provocative exhibition and the demand for recognition.

Thus, in its most conjugal version, homosexuality is a modern category aimed at "normalizing" behaviors and individuals. Even when Foucault demonstrates the value of friendship or love between men, more to seduce than to reassure readers, it is never the structure of the couple that he returns in the end but always the creation of novel relationships. Particularly attentive to the historical dimension of sexuality and the concepts created for thinking about or judging, he never fails to accentuate the modern quality of the vocabulary of "homosexuality," which focuses exclusively on the choice of a partner of the same sex and that greatly differs, for example, from categories commonly used in Ancient Greece. With his work on the historical transformation of concepts used to describe sexual life, the author of *The History of Sexuality* critiqued modern categories. If he did not see in "positive avowal" ("coming out," which consists in publicly declaring and claiming one's homosexuality) the inevitable path toward liberation, it is because he considered neither the very general concept of homosexuality nor the claiming of a homosexual identity as indispensable to the understanding of desire or the experience of new lifestyles. Did he subscribe to a logic of liberation? Nothing is less certain, regardless the role others have wanted to assign him in this respect. As for the tendency to want to construct and have recognized a homosexual lifestyle based entirely upon the traditional conjugal model, with a contract and offspring, I imagine that he would have burst out laughing at it.

In reading, for example, K. J. Dover,[7] Foucault stresses that what matters in the Ancient Greek moral ethic is not a question of a person's choice and their sex, it is the difference between *activity* and *passivity*. In other words, he specifies, between "the fact of penetrating or being penetrated [which are] the two possibilities in the sexual relation." "For the Greeks," writes Foucault, "it is the position of the subject (active or passive) that fixes the great moral boundary. With regard to this constitutive element of an essentially masculine ethic, the options of partners (boys, women, slaves) are of little importance." Thus the connoisseur of boys does not necessarily exclude all commerce with women, and his choices are not the expression of a "particular emotional structure."

This ancient approach is inscribed in an "essentially masculine" ethic, as Foucault emphasizes, since the value of activity is the prerogative of masculinity while passivity falls under the province of femininity. This is why "passivity" here remains shameful for men but not for women. The use of these categories (activity and passivity), insofar as they define masculine and feminine characteristics, implies that roles are inverted in the homosexual relationship: at least one of the two must renounce what he is, and that is why, in this Greek ethic, passivity is shameful for men.

The fact that one of the masculine partners renounces the behavior proper to his sex, that is to say his activity, would suggest that the homosexual relationship thus described sustains a sadomasochistic dimension. The essential dissymmetry present in the difference between partners (active or passive) constitutes an opposition that, if it is not connected with sexual difference, seems overly determined by a relation of power between two men (and indeed, even between two women). In this respect, we might wonder if masochism, often attributed to women by psychoanalysis, is not the effect of a masculine perspective, the perspective of a man who projects onto a woman the shame he would feel were he in her place—and who thus imagines himself as being in her place. Thus, Lacan would not have been wrong in seeing feminine masochism as a masculine fantasy. . . .

These all too brief remarks would not be pertinent here if they did not contribute to the questioning of the activity/passivity opposition we are constantly running up against. Thus one should wonder whether the very use of this opposition, and the meaning it has been given, is not most often derived from a masculine perspective. Because woman experiences gestures and behaviors conforming with her desire as eminently active, and she has no reason to identify activity with virility. Already, the description of maternity has demonstrated the need to critique the usage of these concepts of activity and passivity and the attempt to associate them with masculinity and femininity respectively.

Thus it is not easy to break with the duality of the sexes, nor with the opposition of masculine and feminine. Foucault's approach to homosexuality, interesting though it may be, does not move beyond androcentrism. But it does help to call into question the foundations of and the need for a "homosexual" identity conceived as symmetrical to a "heterosexual" one.

Is it possible or desirable to think of homosexuality as a universal form of sexual desire, for which only the object changes, or should we acknowledge a particular structure, one that does not seek to eliminate its transgressive dimension? The question may be as much theoretical as political. In any case, it is difficult to conceive of a strict equivalence between homosexual and heterosexual models in matters involving procreation. But today this problem is more complex than it seems.

THE DⓄUBLE ⓄRİGİⅡ

The question we keep coming back to, that of *mixity*, allowed us initially to recognize that humankind (*le genre humain*) is naturally divided. In addition, it leads us to question sexual identity as it is cultivated by society—or even as we would like to interpret it—and finally, to examine how mixity structures social life through the institutions regulating the relations between the sexes, principally those of the legal couple and filiation.

The fact that a certain proportion of men and women privilege sexual relations with people of the same sex, and not the other, obviously alters the principle of an interdependence between the sexes. But until the present this did not alter the family, which remained founded on certain rules of kinship and filiation, the most universal being that a child can only issue from a mother and a father—that is, a man and a woman. Whereas now, among the demands homosexuals are making, two deserve special the attention: the creation of the PACS in France, which permits two people to be legally joined according to a contract different from that of marriage but including certain rights and responsibilities, and the possibility for homosexual couples to adopt children or to have children through sperm donations or "surrogate mothers." This second demand raises altogether new questions. If medical procedures allow for more and more artificial ways of having children, by separating parental desire from the biological conditions of childbirth, should everyone be accorded a completely unconditional "right to have a child"? In particular, should a filiation mentioning two fathers or two mothers be established? And can a child be allowed to legally *issue* from two people of the same sex? I say *issue* and not raise because legally, education means nothing precise and doesn't involve the identity of the child.

This recent situation calls for reflection and, if possible, reflection free of taboo.

First of all, the situation in question prompts us to reflect upon the desire for children, its strength, its legitimacy, its universality, to consider the distinction some want to make between erotic choices and the desire to have children. And also, the desire for a "family" life, which may be deeper than we thought. We are generally not disposed to accept certain contradictions and, from a subjective point of view, we prefer to juxtapose our desires rather than to question whether they are compatible. "The unconscious never renounces anything," said Freud. Why renounce procreation if it has become technically independent from all sexual practices?

But beyond subjectivity, we must dare to question our norms, our common principles and values, including those capable of prevailing over certain freedoms, whether they intervene in ethical or personal life or inspire lawmakers. Can we really relegate every ethical, legal, or political problem to the relativism of individual choice? This is very much the question raised, in general, by new techniques in medically assisted procreation.

To the extent that these measures theoretically allow any person to conceive a child, with the aid of donors (of either sperm or eggs), the question has been raised as to whether this technology should be made freely accessible to everyone without exception, or if it must be legally regulated, and how. Beyond the question of individual choices, this raises the questions both of the family structure and the meaning of filiation. It is worth mentioning here Robert Badinter's response at a conference at the Council of Europe in 1985.[1]

The principle this former minister of justice maintains is that we must recognize every human being's "right to give birth" and "freedom to choose the means by which she or he will be able to give birth." Consequently, artificial procreation requires no special legislation—except the prohibition against "taking advantage or profiting from another's body." Apart from this last exception, virtually no criteria seem necessary, and neither age, nor sex, nor the existence of a mixed parental couple are mentioned here. This response is founded exclusively on the rights of man, considered here as the expression of "our conception of man" as well as the principles of our civilization.

Robert Badinter actually refers first to "every person's *right to life*,"[2] which, without the least argumentation, he feels able to understand as the "right to *give* life."* "The right to life *seems* to imply

---

*In French the expression "*donner la vie*" (to give life) is approximately equivalent to the English expression "to give birth." I have chosen to retain a literal translation of "*donner la vie*" throughout this text since the English "to give birth" seems to me more limited in the breadth of its potential meanings, especially as regards the "right" to give life, which in Agacinski's argument applies to men as well as women. *Tr.*

the right of every human being to give life" (my emphasis), this right including "the freedom to choose the means by which he will be able to give life" as well. Badinter then relies on article 8 of the European Convention on the Rights of Man to propose that the "right to intimacy," here again to give it its "full reach," guarantees to everyone the freedom "to make certain decisions *essential for himself*" (my emphasis). Thus the general meaning of this response is to defend the unconditional freedom to procreate, and it is inspired by the necessity to protect each individual's recognized freedom to decide, "within the limited sphere of his intimacies."

Françoise Héritier has responded to this purely individualist conception of freedom and rights by saying, with good reason, that the individual is not an isolated unit, and that the social, in this case forgotten, is not "the simple aggregate of the rights of each of its members."[3] She has also invoked the need to consider the rights *of* the child, especially its right to filiation, side by side with the unconditional right *to* a child.

It is, indeed, quite insufficient, not only from a legal point of view but also from an ethical one, to correlate each human being's decision to give life with a decision that is essential exclusively *for himself*.

From an ethical standpoint, the decision to give life, and then to raise a child, immediately brings with it enormous responsibility that is not necessarily *for myself* (*pour moi*). On the contrary, this responsibility requires me to move beyond my desire and freedom and to question myself as to the freedom and rights of this other for whom I make myself responsible. The decision to procreate, to artificially conceive or adopt a child, is not one of those decisions concerning only *my* subjective freedom, *my* autonomy, or even my *intimacy*; inversely, it is one that requires me to ask myself what I owe to the other. At least if the ethical question is posed, and if the child is not considered as a mere object of desire.

But we are speaking here of a personal ethics, and even if this ethics opens me up to responsibility for another, it could be argued that the legislator has no business in my decision. The fact that this kind of decision involves my responsibility and my most intimate ethical choices does not, however, mean that it should not involve the law.

Unless we consider the ethical dimension to be strictly personal and no concern of society. But if ethics were only personal, what would be the use of creating ethics committees and why should the legislator worry about their opinions? The whole problem of the law is precisely to arrive at an acceptable compromise between shared fundamental values, capable of providing certain ethical "frameworks" that inspire laws, and, on the other hand, to allow for the greatest freedom for each person to choose how to act and live. In this respect, we have, fortunately, stopped legislating questions of sexual mores, with some exceptions, in order to allow individuals their autonomy—considering sexual life as free since it only concerns private life.

But giving life is not so easily separable from ethics and the law, because it involves future beings who, by definition, cannot give their consent, and because, in the the final analysis, it concerns relationships upon which the entire group is constructed—that is, filial relations. So much so that the way in which life is perpetuated and transmitted implies an ethical vision and engages the fundamental structures of our civilization, indeed of all of civilization. It is not by chance that anthropologists are attentive to these questions and reflect upon them. How could the law not be interested in them?

The difficulties, however, are considerable. It is altogether unprecedented that as a result of its scientific knowledge and technical innovations a society finds itself in the situation of calling into question its own traditions or institutions, and even the very foundations of its culture. A society suddenly becomes responsible for an order it inherited ages ago. It is truly the mark of our age to discover, in almost all domains, the infinite field of its responsibility, a responsibility that extends to the world we will leave to our descendants tomorrow. But, paradoxically, this responsibility is also increasingly difficult to define. As they are developed, techniques that should serve our freedom move beyond their aims. Previously, it was a question of *slightly* limiting the role of natural necessity or of accident, holding off death, better mastering births. Today, the possibilities for keeping someone alive artificially or having children born even more artificially have created a situation in which no one knows any longer where the limits of our own power lie.

Nonetheless, regarding this question of the power to give life—and taking into account the ethical point of view and our culture's values—the rights *of* the child cannot be absent from the debate over the right *to* the child. There is even a certain absurdity in speaking of a right *to* the child. Having children is a freedom, but not a right.

The difficulty Robert Badinter's argument raises is that he treats this question of rights only from the angle of defending individual freedoms, with no reference to the ethical and legal dimensions of the problem. By relying solely on the rights of man (the right to "give life" and the right to "intimacy"), he encloses himself in a purely individualistic point of view. This point of view cannot be the only one the lawmaker takes into account. The law does indeed have a normative vocation. It is inspired by values and allows them to be respected. The question here is to know whether our civilization is still capable, in this domain as in others, of escaping its atomization and its exclusive valorization of subjectivity.

It is necessary, then, to extend the debate, especially concerning the child's right to a filiation, even to a generation, which includes him in a human order and makes him something other than a simple laboratory product. Thus, if the freedom to dispose of one's body is limitless and allows the use of surrogate mothers, considered by Robert Badinter as a mere "*adoption through anticipation*" (his emphasis), we must wonder how the poorest women will be protected from the inevitable opening of a marketing of wombs (explicitly condemned by Badinter). The law rarely has the power to prohibit merchandise whose fabrication it has authorized. If a child can become the object of laboratory production and a simple private agreement between the various interested parties, what will keep children themselves from becoming merchandise? It is not clear that we can consider the freedom to *have* children, in the traditional sense of the term, which results from people's private life, and the freedom to *fabricate* children, as is now desired, on the same level. When technology progresses more quickly than reflection, the law may arrive too late.

The use of new technical possibilities is not a matter of fate pure and simple—that is why we are so concerned with preventing human cloning with a reproductive end. In questions of procreation, the law is not obliged to blindly allow the use of every possible technology.

Of course, filiation not necessarily conforming to the conditions of generation is an old story. It seems, however, that the symbolic and legal order of filiation has always retained a certain relation to the natural order of generation. A relationship, at least a mimetic one, exists between these two orders. Even if the family is universally based on legal filiation, our law has increasingly sought to make filiation coincide with genetic origin. This is why the filiation of a child can be legally established, on the child's request, through proof of his origin (through genetic testing for example), even against the will of the father—the mother not being implicated in such procedures. In this case, everything happens as if, in the last analysis, filiation remained based on genetic origin.

Nevertheless, we can grasp the complexity of our legal and moral problems if we recognize, moreover, that genetic origin is stripped of all meaning in order to permit the development of medically assisted procreation techniques. In these cases, the "true parents" are said to be those who desire a child, and the genetic material used, even the maternal "receptacle" necessary for its fabrication, has no significance with regard to filiation. The anonymity of donors is thus carefully protected.

It is a question, in fact, of creating something altogether new, somewhat masked by the image of medicine supposedly just "assisting" procreation and aiding faulty nature. It is a question of passing from natural to artificial procreation, and finally of establishing the possibility of *fabricating* children on the model of artisanal or industrial fabrication. Without a doubt this innovation allows the "sterile couple's" desire for a child to be satisfied. But, having established the principle for this fabrication, it is not surprising that others may want to benefit from the possibility.

From this perspective, the child's right to a filiation established *from his genetic origins* is necessarily abandoned. If not, all adopted children or those born from cell donations would be able to seek out their biological parents.

Thus, we can see that the law recognizes contradictory principles with regard to the foundations of filiation. A child's right to seek out a missing father leads to his genetic origin and, at the same time, the parents' right to adopt or fabricate a child leads to the notion of genes as a simple material for fabrication—a priori foreign to filiation. The law thereby adapts itself to differing strategies and interests. Certain painful cases in the United States have revealed that the rights of a child ordered from the laboratory and the responsibilities of the "parents" pose inextricable problems.

This is why the principles must be unified, by questioning anew the rights of the child, in particular his right to filiation. We must attempt to resolve certain contradictions and to ask ourselves up to what point medical practices and the law should deviate from natural models. To what extent can paternity and maternity be the simple consequences of medical technology and legal constructs?

But can we be sure that setting ethical limits where technology opens effective means for realizing desires is a real possibility?

Everything in modern medical technology is not new, most notably the couple's recourse to a third party to conceive a child. As Françoise Héritier writes, women have always called upon an "external" sire when their husbands were sterile. Likewise, sometimes in the most official of ways, men have had recourse to a woman outside their households when their own wives could not give them a child—like Abraham with his servant Agar when Sarah thought she was sterile. That story, moreover, did not have a happy ending, which proves that these practices already posed problems of filiation and legitimacy. But the fact that another man or woman took the place of the biologically deficient father or mother did not fundamentally affect the mixed structure of the parental couple, which, according to the author of *Masculin/Féminin*, cannot be abandoned without risk.

It is not so simple, however, to establish grounds for caution here, since true filiation, as Françoise Héritier maintains, is institutional and always takes precedence over natural origin. Under these conditions, what would stop new forms of the family from being institutionalized that would allow individuals the total freedom to procreate if they had the technical means to do so? Why not imagine families containing three "fathers" and two "mothers," or any configuration one might wish? If we break with the natural model of procreation, that is, the one that engages two sexed individuals, there really is no reason to stop with two parents. If, hypothetically, parents can be of the same sex, the structure of the couple is no longer necessary.

If these hypotheses defy common sense, it is because it is difficult to imagine an institution not *supported* by nature. The family has always privileged the mixed parental couple because it is inspired by the natural parental couple.

Cultures have always taken many liberties with nature, but they have not been able to or willing to erase the double masculine and feminine origin of every human being—when they become cognizant, of course, of the role of men in procreation. One of the rare examples of a society in which Claude Lévi-Strauss does not recognize the existence of a true family, but merely an economic association, is precisely that of a population that ignores the role of men in procreation. The Wunambal do readily lend their wives to other men, but they have not established any connection, either physiological or legal, between men and children. The latter explains the former. This example confirms that even if the family does not obey a natural law, it is still not a stranger to the *representations* each culture makes of nature.

This leads to the notion that the family, by institutionalizing the mixed parental couple, offers a symbolic representation of origin. This *figuration* of origins demonstrates that filiation cannot be a simple question of cells—but neither is it an arbitrary construct.

The small child, offspring of a human world, must know that she or he descends from a lineage made up of men and women, that is to say, of two concrete figures of a cultivated masculine and feminine humanity and not of anonymous cells or a chain of clones.

One cannot, in fact, abandon this model of procreation: except through cloning, the biological origin of the child is always double, as the unavoidable recourse to cell donors proves. Is it desirable to abandon the model of the mixed parental couple in the establishment of filiation? I do not believe so. In principle, filiation should remain based upon the male and female, masculine and feminine, double origin.

The mixity of humanity, relative to the division of sex roles in generation, is not only a given of physical anthropology but, further, from our point of view, it also structures cultural duality and value by generating singularity and diversity. In effect, it is through the union of the two parents' genes that each individual draws his singularity.

At both the psychological and cultural levels, how does a child, the reputed son or daughter of two fathers or two mothers, define its own sexual identity? If it seemed desirable to create conditions for an increased blurring of the genders, one might overlook this point, but is this the case? It is in the parental couple, as much real as symbolic, that the child discovers the division of man, and thus a form of his finitude and human destiny. It is in the necessary parental complementarity that humans recognize both their difference and their mutual dependence. It is in the impossibility of being *both father and mother* that individuals encounter their own limits, come up against their desire for self-sufficiency, and must assume their sexual identities.

Mixity is a value that is as much fundamental, universal, and ethical as it is biological. Certainly there are many figures of alterity, but the other sex is a fundamental one. The desire to neutralize the very principle of man's double origin will have serious ethical and cultural consequences.

ARİSTOTLE
OVER/AGAİΠST PLATO

It is not by chance that Plato's Republic appears to us today as a "to-talitarian" regime, while at the same time expressing a nonmixed conception of man. In the way in which the lives of the city-state's guardians are organized, the Republic strives to establish a sexually undifferentiated community, by abolishing not the man/woman couple but, rather, the father/mother couple. Whereas, it is precisely the man as father and the woman as mother that constitute the couple that traditionally structures societies.

The Platonic abolition of the family, making way for a "community of women"—in the sense that no man can permanently and exclusively marry one woman—has given rise to abundant commentary over the years. Some have seen here a very "modern" aspect of Plato's thought, one favorable to equalizing conditions between the two sexes. It seems to me, rather, that Plato's thought expresses an effort to reduce the difference of the sexes as much as possible, an effort associated with an indifference toward women and their role, which the Platonic contempt for procreation and apology for the love of boys in *The Banquet* makes more understandable.

This is why, in choosing Aristotle over/against Plato, I would like to suggest that the Platonic utopia makes manifest a dream of communal purity not far removed from Plato's apology for pederasty. There is in Plato a denial of mixity expressed simultaneously by his thinking on love in *The Banquet*, his political thought in *The Republic*, and his metaphysics, with its idealist separation of the sensible and the intelligible. Might not *The Republic* be a homosexual utopia, and might not metaphysics be tied to a fear of the mixed?

Aristotle is usually considered to be one of the most "misogynistic" theorists because in his work the sexes are always strongly hierarchized. However, Aristotle's thought is less formidable than his master's because the founder of the Lyceum is a thinker of mixity, and for him the association between man and woman is at the foundation of politics. Whereas, in an authoritarian move, Plato unifies the city-state and effaces cultural and social sexual difference, creating the gap between the animal part of humans (who copulate and procreate with a view of improving the race) and their political part (devoted to serving the city-state as well as possible).

Indeed, we will recall that Aristotle based the need for the couple on the natural tendency toward generation: "The first necessary union is that of two beings incapable of existing without each other; this is the case for the male and the female with a view toward procreation." Thus, before it applies to humans in general, to the village, or to the city proper, this inability to "exist without each other" pertains to man and woman, because they each want to leave behind a being like themselves. Before all other relationships, it is the interdependence of the sexes that necessitates the mixity of the basic human association—the shared concern over descendants also creating economic, emotional, and political relations.

Thus, Aristotle's *Politics begins* with a politics of the sexes. The interdependence of men and women, the necessity of their coexistence, is at once at the origin of and a principle of the political. Then, to regulate this coexistence comes the necessity for a hierarchical structure defining the family: the familial association institutes the power of the "eldest male," and "every family is governed on the monarchic model."[1] I have previously demonstrated the way in which Aristotle's family is truly a first political association.

This politics reserving all access to citizenship proper for men may be androcentric and unequal. It is preferable, however, to the Platonic utopia because it strives to situate the place of women, while Plato ignores the relations between the sexes in the city-state: the author of *The Republic* grants little value to this union of the two sexes, a union that will seem so necessary to Aristotle.

The difference between the two Greek philosophers' approaches lies essentially in the place and the value each grants generation. For Aristotle, the fact of engendering a descendant responds to a strong human desire in general, while it is, at the same time, the obvious prerequisite for the survival of the city-state. Conversely, for Plato, reproduction is a necessity for the city-state, while it liitle concerns individuals. It concerns them even less if they have more elevated souls.

The question of children is thus seen as a strictly political problem by the magistrates of the Republic. They treat it both from a quantitative point of view, in order to maintain a stable number of citizens, and a qualitative one, in order to select newborns. In the name of a political demand for beauty and quality for the "human race," and as is done in "raising dogs, birds and horses," those who run the city-state must regulate births. The magistrates of the Republic will thus *secretly* organize among the state guardians, through a lottery *they rig*, the union of elite men and women in such a way that only the children of this elite are raised, and not those of the "undesirables." The necessity to proceed secretly and by ruse proves—if this were necessary—that individuals would not spontaneously join together according to these criteria upheld by the magistrates. The fact that Plato assumes the guardians' consent to the procedure of union by lottery reveals to what extent individuals are considered here as a passive herd and confirms the regime's ultra-authoritarian nature.

Children thus conceived will be raised in this city-state by specialized functionaries and must not know their genitors, nor should the latter know their progenitors.[2] For their part, the functionaries who take care of the children must engage "all their ingenuity" to prevent any woman who comes to nurse the babies from "recognizing her own offspring." Instead of familial structure linking one man and one woman, Plato establishes a shared pool of women and children, simultaneously forbidding filiation and marriage, since no man can be linked to one particular woman.

We could regard this abolition of the family as a radical way of freeing women from masculine domination, since it is within the family that the power of each man is traditionally exercised over his wife. Plato can thus serve the cause of women insofar as, in chapter 5 of *The Republic*, he contests any legitimacy of the sexual division of labor. Whether it is a question of making music or making war, the question is not one of sex but of the personal talent of each person. We will have to await John Stuart Mill for a philosopher to again dare to allow women a chance to demonstrate their talents individually. Could Plato have been a feminist ahead of his time? We should never put too much faith in such anachronisms.

In reality, the Platonic indifference with regard to sex as it relates to the distribution of careers and social functions in general comes at the price of a *trivialization* (*insignifiance*) of sexual difference that deserves to be questioned.

From a political point of view, Plato really does consider sexual difference to be no more relevant than the difference between bald people and those who are not bald. Thus there is no more reason to forbid shoe repair to those who are bald than to those who are not, or vice versa, than there is to forbid women a career until now practiced by men. The difference between men and women, like the difference between those who are bald and those who are not, is in reality only a *relative* difference and not an absolute one. It is relative to generation, just as the difference distinguishing those who are bald and those who are not is relative to hair. Even if we are at first tempted to subscribe to the logic of this argument, we must wonder if we must weigh the validity and the consequences of such pure relativity concerning sexual difference. With regard to this difference, Plato is content to say that women "give birth" while men "engender"—which leads us to believe that, in keeping with the Greek vision already expressed by Aeschylus, man is the true generator of the child, even if it is born from the feminine body. Whatever the case, Plato sees nothing in this difference that might justify a reflection on the roles of men and women in the city-state. This is not surprising considering how he regards generation. We could nevertheless contest the validity of the comparison between sex and hair: because (all unconscious associations aside) between those who are bald and those who are not are as many intermediary categories as one might wish. In the lack or loss of hair, all degrees exist. This is why this difference is quite comparable to a difference in color—there too, all nuances are possible—while there is no intermediacy between femininity and masculinity.

As modern as this sexual *indifference* in the Platonic Republic may seem, and as much as certain of our contemporary republicans are again calling for it, we must not confuse this indifference with the idea of an equal status between the two sexes that leaves a place for difference. Nor must we separate it from the whole network of arrangements anticipated by the Republic—that is, the obliteration of the parental couple and the destruction of maternal and paternal ties with their children.

To encourage the equality of the sexes, it might seem useful to deny sexual difference a deciding role in the division of labor. But, by banning the establishment of conjugal and filial ties, it is sexual difference itself that loses all meaning, and the social structure based upon kinship that finds itself excluded. The city-state breaks with the institution of the mixed parental couple, with the family. By making it impossible for biological parents to recognize their children, the city-state also prevents children from recognizing their parents and thus from knowing, through their fathers and mothers, their double, masculine and feminine, origin.

This is certainly only one aspect of this inhuman organization, but the question then arises as to what remains of sexual identity once the maternal and paternal functions, or in other words, the natural and/or instituted ties with descendants, have been eliminated.

On the one hand, it appears that beings who couple according to a lottery and make children with whom they have no relation are regarded as mere cattle. They are masculine or feminine through their genital organs, but they are neither husbands nor wives, neither fathers nor mothers nor even lovers. Thus they are not exactly what we would call men and women. In a more general sense, the organization of the community remains unrelated to sexual difference.

It is not clear whether there are still women or men in this Platonic Republic. We might rejoice in this. But the reduction of difference to its biological function cannot be passed off as the price to be paid for true equality between men and women, because equality cannot have meaning where freedom has none, as is the case here. It is, rather, the sacrifice of individuals to the order of the city-state that explains why their desires and sexual identities have no importance.

A reading of *The Banquet* confirms that of *The Republic* and shows that if reproduction is, above all, a political problem to be treated in a global and authoritarian manner, it is because the individual desire to have children has no value for Plato, unless it is for the "common" who can believe that their desire for eternity may be easily satisfied by the fecundity of bodies. They may well want to leave descendants and "turn toward women," but souls smitten with true love for the eternal will only be satisfied by a love of the truth—that is, the fecundity of souls not of bodies. Men truly seeking eternity thus turn toward the souls the most apt to be elevated, those of boys. And the amorous, if not erotic, relation between master and disciple is far more highly regarded and desirable than the love between man and woman.

We must keep in mind this distinction between the two forms of love and consider this contempt for procreation and women, made explicit in *The Banquet*, in order to understand the absolute indifference with which Plato treats the question of the relations between the sexes and the relationship to children in *The Republic*. The echo of *The Banquet* can be heard wherever the soul defends itself from the body, or the body defends itself from the soul, wherever, in philosophy or eroticism, one separates itself from the other.

The Platonic reduction of sexual difference through the dissolution of the family has the virtue of clarifying—through contrast—a fact anthropologists would confirm, notably that man and woman are not defined only through anatomical or physiological difference.

The masculine/feminine couple is not simply differential; it involves the sexes' relation to a common project—surviving together, providing mortal beings with a future.

Woman's link to man is to a possible companion and a father for her children. Man's link to woman is to a possible partner and mother for his children. It is above all in relation to this *third*, to which they can only give birth together, that man and woman are defined as sexually differentiated beings. If we forget about this relationship to descendants, if we base no social ties upon it—such as marriage and filiation—the difference between men and women no longer has a great deal of meaning and sexual identity itself becomes unimportant. Thus paternity or maternity are the truly decisive proofs of sexual difference, and it is not clear that there are others. As for the child fabricated in a laboratory—the product of the modern, individualist subject, he might be a brother to the orphans of Platonic collectivism: he has no more ancestry.

I have tried to show why, in the end, the Aristotelian hierarchy of the sexes leaves the relation between men and women more open to history than the Platonic utopia with its neutralization of the sexes. Beyond the questions of the family and the city-state, we must propose an ethics of sexual difference. It has rarely been approached philosophically, perhaps only by Emmanuel Lévinas.[3]

This philosopher is one of the very few to have fully adopted the idea of speaking about sexuality as a man and to have done so without identifying the masculine position as that of a universal, nonsexed subject. He poses the question of fecundity beginning with the experience of paternity, thus giving his thoughts an explicitly masculine signature.

The most essential aspect of Lévinas's thought, relative to our question, concerns the way in which he describes fecundity as an event. Far from being merely a technically mastered fabrication—and I might add, even if it is programmed, or even "assisted"—the birth of a child, for him, always transcends any simply subjective project.

Becoming a father, or mother, is not the fact of a desire or a will but the acceptance of an event that moves beyond any mastered decision.

Fecundity is that event that transcends me and opens me to the alterity of that life that comes (that comes from me and from another and with which a free existence begins absolutely). This is why fecundity is a privileged experience of the other.

The meaning of this experience implies that fecundity is not only an anthropological question but truly a fundamental philosophical question, since transcendence of the other can reveal itself therein. Thus the problem is not simply that man and woman cannot exist without each other, although this statement should be understood in its fullest sense. It is knowing what man and woman are responsible for, the one in front of the other, and what surpasses them both, the one and the other.

It is surely what surpasses them both—that is, their descendants—that simultaneously constitutes the cause of their mutual dependence and the stakes of their conflicts.

Politics

WAR OR POLİTİCS

The following definition of war, given at the beginning of the nineteenth century by Clausewitz, is often cited: "War is a mere continuation of politics by other means."[1] Michel Foucault, on the contrary, elaborated the hypothesis according to which political power would be "a war continued by other means than arms and battles."[2] Thus we might think, along with the Prussian general, that the *politics of the sexes* always risks turning into war or, closer to Foucault, that this politics is *still* a "war of the sexes" continued by other means.

I will not maintain either of these two hypotheses, to the extent that there seems to be no symmetry in relations between men and women. Allow me this minor detail: war is a means men use, not women. Thus there is no "war of the sexes."

I like to think that if man invented war, woman invented politics the day—mythical I admit—when she persuaded man to seduce her rather than take her by force as one attacks a citadel. Lacking power and the wish to fight, lacking a love for violence, *I imagine* that in her relations with the other sex, woman developed the art of persuading and governing through the spoken word. It is also most often through the word (*le verbe*) that women are violent, knowing how to manipulate insult, sarcasm, mockery, and humiliation.

Instead of waging war, women have thus endeavored to establish an association with their partners in which each attempted to defend her or his position, something that would not have been possible without a real sheared interest and that is never altogether stable. With their own arms, women have had to struggle against the masculine use of force to dominate women themselves—or to dominate other men. Moreover, we could show that the less men establish political relations among themselves—the more they use pure violence, the less ready they are to negotiate their relations with women. On the contrary, the more a civilization establishes sexual equality, the more it respects individuals.

Any war against women is certainly not ruled out, but it is male violence unilaterally exercised. Certain recent or current barbarous wars, in former Yugoslavia or Algeria for example, involve particularly bloody combat: women and girls raped, forced to bear the fruit of collective violence in their wombs; women and girls hidden, cut off from public life, their throats even slit because they refuse oppression. Muslim fundamentalist terrorism makes war on women as such, not merely to kill women enemies, or the women of the enemy, but to massacre and terrorize those women who resist their own enslavement. Systematically practiced rapes in former Yugoslavia, especially within the framework of Serbian struggles for "ethnic purification," reveal both the racial signification of the conflict and the status of women in this political space.

Women are all the more the object of specific violence, such as rape, when they are considered, by their enemies as much as by their families, as the property of men. Some Bosnian members of the victims' families respond thus to the barbarism of the groups of Serbian soldiers methodically raping women: "Some fathers and husbands want to kill their daughters or wives when they learn of the rape."[3] This unbelievable reaction contributes to the meaning of rape in this war. It is not simply as an enemy that woman is raped but truly as a woman, because she is the enemy's *property*. It is the men that the soldiers humiliate by violating their women. And, without confusing the executioners with their victims, we can see that men, on both sides, have the same relationship to women, that women are goods possessed and that, tainted, they are no longer anything but symbols of shame endured. When the enemy impregnates women and forces them to bear children of "his blood," they become the instruments of ethnic purification. It is the enemy's "race" that he seeks to extinguish through women, to increase his own, as if—a repetition of an old fantasy—the reproduction of "race" passed essentially through the male genitor. This way of violating women is thus inextricable from men's war among themselves. It reveals a more continuous and deeper oppression of women than the one unleashed through war, but this oppression is not necessarily the war's ultimate stake.

In other respects, the absence of symmetry in this war-related violence does not permit us to speak of a "war of the sexes." Though women may be resisters, fighters for their own and their people's freedoms, they are not warriors and have never sought to enslave the other sex. Violent women are always rebels, resisters, revolutionaries, sometimes also terrorists: in general their violence is a counterviolence. Outside these contexts, criminologists have remarked that a man who kills a woman—often *his* woman—takes the violent appropriation of the other to its conclusion, even when he loves her. While the woman who kills, in most cases, completes a process of liberation. She revolts against the one who oppresses her, brutalizes her, imprisons her, or simply suffocates her. These two logics, being hypothetical constructions, don't address the ultimate legitimacy of the actual motive for murder, but they allow us to reflect upon the dissymetry of masculine and feminine expressions of violence.

Violences against women are, as is all too often said to trivialize them, the result of cruelty in general. By unleashing latent human cruelty and collective sadism, war frequently implies sexual violence, and thus rape, thanks to the lifting of the law and impunity. But in certain periods it has also brought with it emasculations in great numbers. Every struggle to the death is accompanied by cruel passions that, in one way or another, lead to rape and mutilation. However, though both sexes may both be the victims of barbarous eruptions, these eruptions are always the work of men. War destroys all "civilized" human relations—including the relations between the sexes—and reduces them to humiliation and destruction. Respect and protection owed to children and the elderly, for example, also disappear under the effect of war-induced madness. Sexual violence in times of war thus should not be considered as revelatory of the relations between the sexes in general. It may be the symptom of a latent oppression and, more generally, the sign of a masculine sadism that finds its expression under certain conditions.

As for crimes committed against women in times of peace, their particular nature harshly refutes the illusory discourses on who knows what sort of erasure of sexual difference. Here it would be necessary to return to criminological works and their analysis from the angle of the difference between men and women.[4]

Although violence is certainly not the key to the relations between men and women, it is decisive in approaching the difference between them. No reflection on the two sexes can ignore that there is a difference between them in terms of behavior and strength. A simple observation of children's behavior suffices to show that girls are—in general—less violent, less aggressive, and also weaker than boys—something that is also evident in women. That is why, despite certain exceptions, a man does not feel a priori threatened by a woman; this normally tends to inhibit his aggressivity, but it also gives him the potential to use his physical superiority to satisfy his sexual drives or simply to subjugate the other sex. Initially, this difference probably rendered women more fearful; at the same time it explains women's ambivalent relation to men, a mixture of fear and trust with regard to one who might either threaten or protect. The relative fragility of women, heightened during the time they carry children—that is to say, in fact, a quite limited period of time—has increasingly fewer consequences in modern life, but nevertheless, it can be neither ignored nor neglected.

The idea that relations between the sexes are of a *political* nature, in the broadest sense of the term, helps us to think beyond the two main conceptions of gender: one based completely on nature and the other explaining gender essentially through culture. The cultural conception presents the advantage of leaving space for a transformation of traditions and institutions, in such a way as to free women by giving them a new status. But what status? Will it be entirely constructed, or will we witness a complete obliteration of genders? We have often gone too far with the idea that gender is entirely constructed: to the point of confusing femininity with class membership, and to the point of making feminine identity the simple effect of a relation of domination. Certainly, a social culture of difference exists—the genders thus have a permanently artificial character—but artifice is supported by natural elements, and women have also contributed, with what they were or what they wanted to be, to the creation of their own femininity, giving it its variable forms and aspects.

To say that the relations between men and women have always been more or less political is to admit that the two sexes have written a history of their relations, each one with the means at its disposal and each through striving to attain its ends and defend its interests. Women would have been truly cowardly if for centuries they had accepted being the passive victims of men. If they have won certain freedoms and have claimed certain rights only in very recent times, it is because they lacked the means and because freedom, in the modern sense, existed for no one. In the past, women's interests were dependent upon their belonging to a social order or a class. There is never absolute and atemporal freedom for any category whatsoever. Taking circumstances into account, it is not only the means that have changed but also the possible ends. Any strategy is contingent upon circumstances and incorporated within an overall historical situation.

The fact that, as women, we now fight for this or that freedom, this or that status, does not mean that one or the other freedom was owed to us for all eternity—as if, paradoxically, forms of freedom were as programmed as those of nature. In reality, there is no single and definitive form of freedom but only ways, particular for each individual, to become aware of what she or he wants or no longer wants. Sartre was right in speaking of freedom in terms of invention, but we do not invent *out of nothing*, and the *situation* out of which we invent our freedom includes a great number of determinants, including natural and historical givens. Thus "freedom" is itself a modern concept, and it is forever transforming.

To speak of the political relations between the sexes is also to say that these relations are open, subject to perpetual transformations; stakes in ever merging strategies. Without absolute reference points, without ultimate truth. Each person, with his own strategy, takes part in the game, and no one can escape it to reveal, completely naked, the true relationship between men and women. There isn't a neutral (*neutre*) position in the politics of the sexes any more than there is sexual neutrality. Isn't politics in general, and not only the politics of the sexes, what places all of us in a closed field of forces where the possible goals and actions are not infinite? This phenomenon of *closure* excludes any absolute point of view.

Each person only conducts his or her politics, more or less consciously, beginning from an overall situation in which the fact of being sexed plays a part. The politics of the sexes thus begins with this basic psychology, which means that each person, man or woman, is conscious of a natural difference that the transformations of history do not suppress and that must be taken into account in any relation to the other. The egalitarianism that claims to be based upon the identity of the sexes and seeks only equal rights is naïve: *equity* is more just, since it takes into account the role of the difference between them as it takes into account certain differences between individuals. We could not, for example, treat children, adults, and the elderly equally.

Whatever the case, the two sexes are not a priori enemies. To the contrary. Everywhere and always, men and women have united: as oppressive as forms of union may have been for women, it is not through disunion that they have wanted to free themselves.

Let us go even further. The originality of the relations between the sexes may reside precisely in the fact that *war between them is impossible*. Too dependent upon each other for the satisfaction of their inclinations, they have been forced to associate with each other, and it is the impossibility of war that has condemned them to politics. Between war and politics, it is less a question of a continuity or a transformation than an alternative: *either* war *or* politics.

The mutual dependence of the sexes is incompatible with the logic of war, which can lead to the wish to annihilate the enemy. Never, to this day, has one sex wanted to make the other disappear.

Until the present, inequality between men and women seems to have been the rule, but this does not mean that women have not endlessly negotiated their status. Similarly, men have not been able to appropriate women and children for themselves without obtaining, *as much as possible*, women's consent. It is this obligation to negotiate a relation at once natural, necessary, and conventional, where need, solidarity, and divergent interests mix, that gives the relation between the sexes its political dimension.

ARCHAİC AND
LİBERTİNE FRANCE

The motif of a *politics of the sexes* became all the more obvious to me—while I was seeking to understand the fate of feminism today—when events of the spring of 1996 brought into the foreground the problem of women's place in politics and thus the problem of the relation between men and women at the heart of public life.

In this respect France has combined the most modern and the most archaic conceptions. Supposing that there could be one elsewhere, which is far from certain, there will be no war of the sexes in France: perhaps because here we like friendship and love, seduction, and even licentiousness (*libertinage*) too much. Men and women, here even more than elsewhere, have always sought to understand and please each other, and they have not been above borrowing from each other the qualities that might have been lacking in their own sex: a man with no grace or a woman with no character would bore us.

And then, France finds puritanism repugnant; this is well known. Relations between men and women have always occupied a large space here, and sexual commerce itself is rather free. To some extent we apply the principle of secularity to sexual and love life: as with religious affairs, sexual affairs are strictly private. One might say, parodying Condorcet, that they are left "to the conscience of each individual." Aside from matters involving violence or minors—or the definition of conjugal responsibilities—the law does not concern itself with people's sex lives, and this aspect of private life is legally protected. More easily than elsewhere, public opinion itself distinguishes the judgment of public personalities for their talent or competence, in whatever domain, from any consideration of the choices they make in their private, and especially, their sex lives. It is not that the public lacks curiosity on this subject, but, while it may find entertaining what the interested parties themselves make visible or public, it would consider disgraceful investigations by the press or the desire to discredit someone in public life by dredging up his private life. Here, we cannot imagine that an individual's morals could destroy his career (such as, in other countries, marital infidelity or homosexuality). I am idealizing a bit, no doubt, but there exists in this domain a consensus favoring secrets . . . from which, it is true, women still do not benefit as much as men. However, for a long time, first in the aristocratic world and later in other circles, women have demanded sexual freedom. The difference from Anglo-Saxon countries is considerable here. Still today, a very pc English political theorist finds it astonishing that in France we like to speak of "seduction" and that, at the same time, we refuse the notion of "date rape,"[1] as if seduction were already a first step toward rape. . . . How to translate "date rape" into French? Let's say: rape by a friend, someone with whom a woman had a date.

But what is incomprehensible to us, on the contrary, is that someone might see a relation between seduction and rape. If seduction consists in arousing desire in the other, it is the opposite of rape and need not resort to it. If rape is compelling someone by force to submit to sexual relations, it is because this person is not at all consenting and obviously has not been seduced. Seduction and rape reciprocally exclude each other. Rape facilitated by a date is thus, simply, rape, without excuses, in response to which one might say, however, in certain cases, that the victim should have avoided putting herself in a situation of isolation and risk if she had already decided not to let herself be seduced. To emphasize this risk-taking is not to accuse the victim of "provocation," nor to attribute to her responsibility for the crime of which she is the victim; rather, it is to recall a dissymetry of situation that it is naïve and dangerous to neglect. Politics begins here. That man's desire can be, at times, impetuous, even violent, is a matter of basic clearheadedness that our grandmothers already possessed. The awareness of the difference in masculine and feminine sexual behaviors is one of the elements, in private relations, basic to a politics of the sexes, to which belongs the following question: How to seduce or, depending upon the case, avoid being seduced? But if, in confusing equality and similitude, we believe it possible to negate all difference and make men act like women and women like men, we expose ourselves to a great many disappointments.

The question posed to French women by our English political theorist contains another element: a condemnation of seduction as such, no doubt because the idea of seduction already contains the loss of absolute self-mastery, a certain self-abandon, and this element of abandon seems contrary to the ideal of autonomy that, in general, drives ideologies of emancipation, and above all women's emancipation. In amorous abandon, either emotional or physical, some have been quick to see a figure of an old feminine passivity. In reality, whoever is seduced, man or woman, to a certain extent, no longer decides his or her own desire and loses a part of his or her autonomy. This loss is a part of love and, if we love love, speaking as Stendhal or Saint Augustine, we agree to renounce absolute autonomy without seeing that as the mark of alienation or a rejection of freedom. And furthermore: even if it were a question of such a renunciation, betting once more on our singularity, we would respond that we want to keep our freedom to be seduced—and to seduce.

To close these remarks on French women, perhaps more serious than they seem, I will say that in our country we do not entertain a Manichean vision of sexual difference and, as Mona Ozouf rightly emphasizes, we do not claim to oppose "collectively guilty men to collectively victimized women."[2]

However, taking this "French singularity" into account will not lead me, unlike Mona Ozouf, to be satisfied with an abstract universalism, inherited from the Enlightenment and Jacobinism, which is supposed to characterize "French genius" and define for us the soul of democracy. It is not that I am rejecting the principle of "the equivalence of individuals," nor that I am disputing the quite praiseworthy tendency among French women to see themselves "first as free and equal individuals"[3] but, rather, that I am not sure that this vision of themselves has ever sufficed, any more today than yesterday, to assure them the enjoyment of the freedoms to which they aspire.

I would not be forcibly shocked if one said, along with George Sand, that "a man and a woman are really the same thing," under the condition that women are not alone in thinking it and saying it.

"Protected by such a conviction," continues Mona Ozouf, in speaking of French women, "they experience sexual difference without resentment, cultivate it with happiness and irony, and refuse to essentialize it."[4]

Alas, this good use of difference and this happy combination of a universal equality of rights and a peaceful cultivation of difference are undermined by the continuance of customs or behaviors tending to perpetuate the rules of masculine communities—in particular in political life.

As much as the relations between the sexes *in private life* often seem full of charm and freedom, in other spheres the French are conservatives and traditionalists. On one hand, we rejoice in our singular freedom of mores; on the other, we come up against a truly archaic reality.

Confident about their egalitarian convictions and their rights, most French women engaged in political life have discovered themselves to be the objects of deeply rooted prejudices. They have even found themselves treated in a vulgar manner because of their sex. The old French courtesy quickly reveals its limits when women venture out of their traditional roles and call their place and their status into question. Those women who believed they could act freely *as individuals* were barred, jeered at, and at times insulted, *as women*: "Obscenity is the daily bread of women in electoral campaigns," writes Elisabeth Guigou.[5] The numerous painful anecdotes, which women dare to bring up today, are not mere accidents. They reveal a tenacious state of mind, as well as the difficulty in getting everyone to recognize "the equivalence of individuals," independent of their sex.

Consequently, as much as we might want to reject the idea of "essentializing" sexual difference—and this is not the main concern of our political women—it is difficult not to question the irony they become the object of *as women*[6]—in a village meeting as on the benches of the National Assembly. The allusion to the fact that a woman militant or candidate would be more at home in her kitchen than at a public meeting, the overly frequent insult identifying the political woman with a "whore"—these affronts cruelly remind us that the general mentality, in all circles, has still not really gained a very clear consciousness of the equality of individuals. Dear to republicans, the *French genius*, completely imbued with universalism and indifferent to distinctions of sex, is theoretically seducing, but in practice, not yet all that widely received. . . .

Off-color aggressiveness is not, moreover, the only way to neutralize women on the political front. There are much more serious tactics. Those women who aspire to a position of responsibility encounter enormous difficulties, due both to their life situations (notably when they have children) and to a fierce resistance on the part of political parties, which continue for the most part—especially, though not surprisingly, on the right—to consider the public domain as reserved for the "stronger sex."

Hence, this *French archaism* that, from the moment women were given the vote, only in 1944,[7] up to the ridiculously low proportion of women in the National Assembly today,[8] poses questions to us as female citizens and, in a larger sense, to French society as a whole.

It is this archaism's formidable resistance to any evolution toward concrete equality that leads French women at the present moment to be no longer content with relying on equality before the law. They recognize that this theoretical equality constitutes, in practice, the best possible cover for the continuation of misogynist traditions and inequalities. This is why they are demanding, *as women*, a real sharing of power with men.

Thus it is not by chance that the question of the place of women has been reopened within the context of political life—even if it is obviously not limited to this context—and that, in our country, elected women, or formerly elected women, put forward the Manifesto of the Ten for parity in June 1996.[9] It had been preceded, one month earlier, by the Charter of Rome,[10] which vowed to promote "the equal participation of women and men in places of power, influence, and decision in all spheres of society." It was signed by women, ministers of different European countries. These initiatives have marked what we can hail as a new step in *women's politics.*

Without denying the other dimensions of their involvement, European women are invoking an ideal of parity and calling for equality *between* men and women in instances of decision. They are thus exposing an entirely original crisis in democracy. The situation itself is not new, since women never have had true access to power in the Republic. What is new, however, is that their underrepresentation in political institutions *now* appears as an unacceptable scandal, and public opinion itself experiences this underrepresentation as a crisis in democracy.

We must now examine the validity of this diagnosis and see if this crisis calls for reforms or, at a deeper level, rethinking representation and developing a new conception of equality and democracy.

EQUALITY

However universal sexual difference may be, it tells us nothing of what should be done with it in terms of the practical organization of human beings. It does not bring with it, *in itself*, any particular institution, any segregation, any hierarchy of any order—economic, social, political, religious, or other. The *hard pedestal* of anatomical and physiological differences suggests, perhaps, types of behavior linked to the search for pleasure or parental drives, but it can program nothing on the institutional, legal, or social orders.

Shouldn't we say, at least, that the two sexes are naturally equal? Certainly, on the condition of defining what is meant by "naturally," and thus emphasizing the *political* nature of the idea of equality. This point will allow me to show that the political value of equality does not rest on the classical idea of *truth*. I would like to emphasize, in addition, that *equality* must not be confused with *identity*. To say that men and women are equal does not mean that they are identical: thus the principle of equality does not exclude the recognition of difference.

We will say that equality bears no relation to a universal truth, empirical or rational in origin, and that it is not a matter of *knowledge*, since it cannot be demonstrated to be true or false. As unnerving as this renunciation of truth may appear, it is inevitable as soon as justice is not a simple effect of nature and becomes a question of institutions. Hannah Arendt said the same thing about the equality of men in general: it is neither evident nor demonstrable.[1] Despite the paradoxical expression of the 1789 Declaration of the "Rights of Man," which affirms that "men *are born* free and equal of rights," an equality *of rights* is necessarily the product of institutions and not of nature. There really is a paradox, because *birth* seems to suggest a natural, even native state, whereas an equality *of rights* is necessarily *instituted*. The paradox is erased if it is understood that henceforth men *will be born* free and equal in a *new legal order*, beginning from the moment when these rights have been solemnly *declared and recognized* by a constituent authority, and that this equality will no longer be contestable. Thus the equality of rights is not a natural, immediate given but, we might say, it becomes "natural," or universal, through the very act of the Declaration—which is understood to apply to all of humanity. The fact of "being born" with equal rights does not refer to a natural state of equality but is opposed to the legal order of the *Ancien Régime*, in which "birth" meant each person's *social* condition and depended upon his family origins. So, men *were born* with *more or less* rights. Equality seems to draw its source from nature because it destroys an established and unjust order. In fact, it establishes another order, which is no more natural but appears more just.

Thus the institution of equality is not the necessary consequence of a demonstrable or evident truth but the result of a political decision. Invoked from a legal or moral point of view, the principle of equality refers to the *recognition of a value* and not the *knowledge of a fact*. By saying that men are equal in dignity, one posits that dignity should be equally respected by all, regardless of all sorts of differences between them. If it is established that everyone should have equal rights, the principle of a universal relation to the law having nothing to do with identity is instituted. To this extent, equality is not directly related to the concepts of resemblance and difference. To be objectively valid as a principle, it must above all be recognized by the legitimate "constitutive" authority or authorities.

The same goes for the equality of the sexes (or for the statuses given to men and women at any time): it is a moral and political principle, corresponding to a moment in the history of the politics of the sexes. But who decides the justness of the principles ruling a society?

In a modern democracy such as our own, it is both at the heart of public opinion and through democratic, political expression that values are recognized and principles posited—on the political scene. Values are no longer the expression of an absolute or transcendent power (such as God or Nature) as in the past but the expression of a dominant will or the compromise resulting from the relation of forces present on the "playing field." As with a sporting event, only one of the teams present, and no other, can claim victory, even if there were some ideal, supposedly excellent, team. This means that political forces must elaborate theories capable of legitimating their strategies and, inversely, that political ideas that seem more just must find or assemble forces capable of supporting and implementing them. Today, the place of men and women in society is changing, thanks in part to democratic political forces and the principles in the name of which they act.

Once women became aware of the need to transform their condition and to take actions toward this end, discrepancies manifested themselves at the heart of their emancipation movements. Thus, in the nineteenth century, two opposing kinds of strategies emerged: one that focused on gaining civil rights, and one that made gaining citizenship a priority. Hubertine Auclert fought for the latter, the potential to vote on laws seeming to her the key to everything else. Feminist movements were divided, inevitably, as are all political struggles, because it was necessary to establish objectives and choose strategies. What objectives should women assign themselves today? Should they demand only equality? This principle can't be invoked without bringing up a few questions.

Often, rather than upholding the principle of equality in difference, the egalitarian claim called upon a *common human identity*, as if the identity and the similarity among people ought to be the basis for equal rights.

The same reasoning is used to fight racism: we appeal to identity as a stronger basis for equality. However, it is better to recognize this empirical fact: all men are not the same—and even less so men and women—humanity is diverse and not uniform, and it is better to attempt to understand and regulate the conflicts inherent in this diversity. Diversity is not simply racial, as was believed in the nineteenth century; the traits partially shared by a group are not at all stable. The mixing of populations and the vagaries of genetics create a situation wherein there are no two identical individuals: the core of the individual is her or his singularity. But populations do have or acquire common characteristics, and coexistence with *others* is not easy, each—group or individual—being *the other* for the others.

The "universalist," humanist point of view is often valorized, which translates into the famous expression: "Nothing human is foreign to me."[2] But it is incorrect. An opening to tolerance would be better based on an inverse principle, according to which we accept that the human is so often and so profoundly foreign to us. If we recognized that the human is so often foreign to us, and that it is nevertheless necessary to respect it and live with it in peace, everyone would be better equipped to confront sexism and racism. Living together rests upon the ability to compromise, never upon the presupposition of a natural harmony.

Difference, thus, is not the opposite of equality but, rather, of identity: two things are either identical or different, even if one object can be identical to another from a certain perspective and different from another perspective. Thus man and woman are different through certain characteristics and the same through others. As for *equality*, it's opposite is inequality, not difference.

In terms of the law, to say that men are equal does not mean that they are identical. Confusion arises because the word "identical" is sometimes used in the same sense as "equal," especially when equality refers to a quantity. We say, for example, that the volume of one container is *equal* or *identical* to that of another.

Today, the equality of persons means the equality of their civil or political rights and not the fact that these persons are identical to each other through their nature or even their condition.

The eighteenth-century encyclopedists, like the revolutionaries themselves, were careful to distinguish between the moral equality of citizens and their difference in nature or condition, their inequalities in situation or fortune. After the Revolution, the differences or inequalities in condition were no longer supposed to justify certain inequalities of rights: this alone was new. A poor person could become, from the point of view of rights, the *equal* of a rich one, but this did not change the "inequality" of their incomes. In this sense, not only are equality and differences not contradictory, they define a system. Moreover, the equality of certain rights posited by the Declaration of the "Rights of Man" assumes and maintains inequalities *of fact* and of condition. This is very well known.

This is why civil and political rights have had subsequently to be extended to all, most notably to women, and supplemented with social rights regarding economic and material life, fighting poverty, and justly aiming to reduce inequalities in condition. To what extent can we accept these inequalities? Are there not human situations that require specific laws? What does a law guaranteeing security mean for a man who has neither work nor housing? What does freedom of opinion mean for someone who receives no education? The overly formal nature of the rights of man has been rightly criticized. These rights were necessary and fundamental—but not sufficient. The idea of justice cannot be limited to that of equality.

Thus we must ask ourselves if the unequal condition between the sexes must not be corrected by laws or measures that also move beyond the abstract and formal equality of all individuals. The abstract equality of rights has, furthermore, revealed its limits with regard to women. First, of course, because the principle itself, at its inception, did not at involve all women. Regarding civic rights, for example, a judgment of the 1885 Court of Cassation reminds us that women were initially excluded from the right to vote while it was based on the poll tax, and that, when it became "universal" in 1848, "the Constitution has not extended to others than citizens of the male sex who, until then, were the only ones invested with it, the right to elect the representatives of the country." Women had a great deal of difficulty, as we know, in winning equal civic rights. But even after having obtained them, it was clear that it changed few habits and left intact the masculine monopoly over power, especially in France.

That is why feminism's "egalitarian" tendency has had to be fulfilled through struggles for the actual application of rights and through specific demands. It is well known that, in the work world as in politics, equality cannot be taken for granted, not even that which should guarantee equal pay for equal work. In economic life, a large proportion of women remain underpaid and very few manage to attain positions of power.

It is necessary to recognize the limits of equality when it remains too abstractly considered: the strict equality of the law, and the fact of blindly applying the same law to cases that are by nature incomparable, can lead to injustice. The need for equity must allow for correcting, or even surpassing, the simple application of the general law in its way of rendering justice, taking measures or making decrees, and even making laws, by taking into account the concrete reality of cases.

If, in principle, an equality of rights ignores the differences between people, it would be unjust that certain rights be applied equally to all. The enjoyment of numerous rights is thus subject to certain conditions, such as age, the fact of not having a criminal record, or having full mental faculties. Accordingly, certain measures are just and equitable, although they are not equally applied to the two sexes: maternity leave, of course, the interdiction of certain kinds of work (such as those requiring the use of a pneumatic drill). . . . Taking sexual difference into account in law and institutions thus appears just and obliges us to recognize the limits of an abstract equality.

Although, strictly speaking, equality runs contrary to all discrimination, certain exceptions are nonetheless admissible under the law. This is the case in the domain of social law. Certain rights are reserved for particular categories—family, the retired, the ill, children, the disabled, the unemployed. Others are assigned as a function of a person's resources. These rights are necessarily "discriminatory," since they must *compensate* for inequalities, correct them, or help the most disenfranchised.

The limits of equality can be verified in another domain, that of the *equality of opportunity*, a popular expression and an extension of the principle of equality as stipulated in article 6 of the Declaration of the Rights of Man with regard to equal eligibility for public employment: "All citizens . . . are equally eligible for all public employment, positions, and promotions, according to their capacities, and without any distinction other than their virtues and their talents."

France is particularly attached to this equal "eligibility," or "equal opportunity," which plays a part in the system of republican elitism: equality gives everyone the chance to bid for any given post or employment, to be admitted to a process of selection that then chooses the most competent. The system has been proven; it is tied to the idea and practice of competitive examinations and opposes the just distinction of merit to former favors and arbitrary appointments (which does not mean that a free appointment is necessarily a favor: it can sometimes respect the criterion of merit just as well as an anonymous selection). Even outside public employment, equality today theoretically forbids all a priori discrimination regarding "applicants" for employment, a post, or even the purchase of an apartment, most notably for reasons of religion, origin, or sex.

The rejection of all discrimination explains the mistrust the use of quotas can provoke in our country, to the extent that a quota is a "positive discrimination." In effect, it institutes the obligation to include in a group a minimum number of individuals defined a priori: for example, women. Intended to correct an injustice that simple equality is powerless against, the quota does seem, however, to be a measure of equity in certain cases.

But discrimination, even *positive*—since it seeks to correct an exclusion and not, in principle, to institute one—is contrary to the principle of equal rights, or equality before the law, which should be "the same for all, whether it protects or punishes" (article 6 of the Declaration of the Rights of Man).

It is appropriate, then, to consider a few nuances here. In particular to distinguish between the cases in which eligibility is a matter of a verifiable competence, as, in principle, with competitive examinations and cases in which the assessment of talents and virtues is much more subjective, as with the listing of candidates on an electoral roll. We do not make this distinction often enough, and thus, certain men, and moreover, certain women, candidly believe that you become a candidate in an election because of competence.

What women are really rejecting, with just pride, is being made the objects of a "complacent" selection system based on criteria that would be less stringent than would be applied to their masculine counterparts. Women are loath to use quotas when it is a question of selection according to specific or verifiable knowledge and expertise. They are right, provided that the selection criteria are well-defined, quantifiable, and do not otherwise conceal sexist criteria. This cannot always be taken for granted.

The equitable use of quotas can prove necessary to counterbalance covert discrimination, for example, the a priori privileging of boys, without admitting it. It can compensate for a flagrant inequality in *access*, even to eligibility itself. It can also be useful to institute mixity where it did not previously exist, or within groups not based on criteria of competence, such as electoral rolls.

Internalizing a sexist prejudice, many women wonder if it is truly possible to find "worthy" female candidates to fill 30 or 50 percent of the electoral rolls, without asking themselves if the 95 percent of male candidates in municipal elections, for example, have been the objects of a rigorous and impartial selection based upon their "worth." Doubting themselves, women feel that if the decision was made to present a certain number of women candidates, they would not necessarily be good enough. . . . We do not see men exhibiting such scruples, and they are right not to, because it is the voters who should, finally, judge their merits. And because, and educators have sufficiently verified this, intellectual aptitude is completely equal between girls and boys. As for other qualities we might expect from any given candidate for political responsibilities, they are a matter of experience and moral virtues: courage, loyalty, tenacity, honesty, respect for the other, and still other qualities hardly assessable through usual modes of selection.

Access to candidacy is thus an excellent example of a domain where voluntarist measures, even legally imposed, on the part of political parties are justified and warrant the use of quotas for women.

The problem of equal *access to candidacy* is posed elsewhere. Even before any intentional discrimination, equal opportunity for boys and girls, men and women, can only come about if, first, both groups can apply for studies, positions, employment. . . .

When we move from a world closed to women to a progressive opening of doors, sector after sector, we cannot expect any sort of immediate equality, either of opportunity or of performance. The weight of habit and tradition, the influence of families, the timidity of women just starting out, all these things will continue to limit girls' and women's ambitions. To borrow an analogy from logic (as competitive exams are not lotteries): everyone who buys a lottery ticket can *equally* win, but everyone does not buy a ticket. In a society from which they have so long been excluded, girls will not immediately buy their tickets for the future.

That is why when secondary school teaching opened to women,

it wouldn't do to grant them the right to studies and competitive exams: little by little, in several disciplines, two competitive exams for secondary teachers were created: one for women and one for men—it being understood that an equal level of competence was expected from both groups, a level guaranteed by the jury. The existence of this double competition amounted to the organization of an approximate parity of recruitment of secondary school teachers until the end of the sixties. This was the equivalent of instituting a quota of approximately 50 percent for women.

Finally, we are often unaware that the exclusion of women was, first of all, simply the reverse of a "positive discrimination" traditionally benefiting men. A discrimination so ancient and powerful that it was forgotten. For centuries, men in Western societies formed a true "caste," monopolizing most social activities and powers. Winning equality between men and women necessarily involved the dissolution of this caste, but this could not be accomplished quickly.

During the period when certain careers were opening up for young women, masculine recruitment continued to be more or less privileged. It was not so long ago that the jury of a secondary teaching exam in philosophy, at the time of the oral reviews, privately admitted recruiting a majority of men "so as not to feminize the body of philosophy teachers too much." It was admitted, here as elsewhere, that a career that became *feminized* simultaneously became *devalued*. Maintaining a majority of men thus passed as a way to defend a discipline or a career.

The notion of competence must also lead us to pose certain questions—for example, in the area of the social sciences. Certainly, intellectual qualities can be evaluated and resolved around the singularity of a career, a work, or a person. It is not a question of making a judgment a priori taking someone's sex into account; it is a question of understanding that it is important that both men and women practice the social sciences. Because it would be naïve to believe in the existence of a sexually neutral scientific truth, independent of the perspective of the observer. Sexual difference is one of the "objects" studied in anthropology, psychoanalysis, and elsewhere, but it also affects the "subjects" of these sciences, who are not pure, disembodied thought but, rather, concrete individuals. Anthropology, history, psychology and psychoanalysis, economics, political science, philosophy, etc. are not the work of neuter subjects but of men and women whose points of view depend in part on their own conditions and on their own experiences as sexed beings. Their points of view, at least on certain subjects, cannot be absolutely "objective." This may be why, until today, androcentrism has characterized most theories on the family, procreation, the social and economic orders, and the unconscious. Androcentrism reigns in philosophy as well.[3] This is why, since it is impossible to escape our condition or the differential structures it generates, we must accept the always "political" dimension of these sciences, acknowledge this *unconscious politics of the sexes*, and avoid granting the masculine perspective a monopoly on the interpretation of all things human.[4] Which means that women must actively contribute to the theoretical work in these fields, which they do remarkably well today, with no a priori, and without, of course, enclosing themselves within a militant bias. This is not the goal of knowledge. The shift in perspective should be achieved with the greatest integrity and by seeking to acknowledge sexual difference—in other words, by considering the duality of most human facts.

Finally, given equal competencies, comparable talents, it is good that we combine the differentiated experiences of men and women in society and that most functions, tasks, and responsibilities are not locked up in a *monosexual* universe. The presence of women at all levels of the hierarchy is in the process of changing the world of the police as much as that of the social sciences. But the goal is not to create feminine monopolies. It is regrettable that primary school teaching is becoming the exclusive domain of women. Men would be perfectly within their rights to request that positions in grade schools be reserved for them. The ideal is not a confrontation between masculine and feminine claims but the shared recognition of the value of mixity.

Thus we can see that voluntarist measures, such as quotas, can be equitable when it is a question of opposing monopolies. As legitimate as quota strategies may be, they are a bit different from the idea of parity. For some, a quota policy aims especially at correcting how society and democracy function and at somehow improving the manner in which the principle of equality is applied. For others, quotas should allow us to approach parity pragmatically, the idea, that is, of an equal allocation of responsibilities or functions.

Parity in politics has thus taken on the meaning of a power sharing between men and women that calls for a new definition of democracy. In France, the ill will political authorities have often shown toward attempts to open political life to women potentially drives the most reformist among them to the path of radical parity. For example, in 1982, in the face of dramatic exclusion of women from political life (an exclusion of fact, not of law), Gisèle Halimi proposed an amendment requiring every electoral list to not have more than 75 percent candidates "of the same sex." We remember what followed: the two assemblies voted for the amendment, but the constitutional council, seizing this text, declared it unconstitutional and annulled it, on the grounds that it divided the voters or those eligible into categories. This decision, legally contestable, is even more contestable politically.

"Perhaps it is the ruse of reason that always leads France to adopt more radical solutions than those of neighboring countries," Blandine Kriegel judiciously remarks.[5] This specialist in political philosophy has perfectly understood that if, in matters of sexual equality, "the method of small steps" and positive discriminations continue to meet with fierce resistance in France, the only other option will be to opt for the most radically effective political solution: parity.

PARİTY

The idea of parity was put forward for the first time by one of the most audacious French feminists, Hubertine Auclert, the very same woman who in 1880, in a letter to the prefect, refused to pay her taxes as long as she could not vote: "I leave to the men who enjoy the power to govern the privilege of paying the taxes they vote for and distribute as they please. . . . I have no rights, thus I have no burden. I do not vote, I do not pay."[1] The argument's strength struck public opinion but was not enough to move the parliament nor, moreover, women in general who were more preoccupied with the attainment of civil rights. A few years later in 1884, Hubertine Auclert again demanded that the supposedly "universal" suffrage be extended to women and at the same time suggested that the assemblies be composed of "as many women as men."

In a single move, this demand situated itself on an entirely new plane. It was not simply a question of putting an end to the masculine monopoly on democratic and republican power[2] and abolishing the exclusion of women from the state by giving them the right to vote or be elected. It was a question of a completely unheard-of idea: that of men and women sharing political power. For Hubertine, it went without saying that the political equality she was calling for must mean the recognition of women *as such* as the other part of the sovereign people. Men and women should thus constitute, *together and equally*, the body of the electorate as well as that of the elected.

This utopic vision, then, of power sharing between the sexes is the one reappearing today. Not, it seems, under an inevitably arithmetic form, but as a demand for a balance of men and women among the leading authorities. This vision is what, in 1996, inspired the Charter of Rome and the Manifesto of the Ten. It is this vision, again, that informs public opinion when there is unanimous outrage at the very small number of women in the National Assembly and the Senate—about 5 percent in 1996!—and when it is declared desirable for women and men to participate equally in decision making. Numerous polls attest to this trend in public opinion. Even more: the gap between the principle of equality posited by the law and the reality of political fact, showing the law to be almost exclusively masculine, is everywhere denounced.

But it would be wrong, in this case, to oppose the equality of rights to the reality of facts. Equality only implies, as we have remarked, that rights are *the same* for women and for men (the right to vote and to be eligible to hold office). The equality of men and women *before the law* has never meant that there should be as many women as men electors or elected—that is, a quantitative equality *between* men and women. Obviously, there are *approximately* as many women electors as men—and even a few more—as a result of the approximately equal distribution of the population between men and women. On the other hand, as it is beginning to dawn on us, there are almost no women elected in France. Is it a question, as we often hear said, of a "scandalous" functioning of our institutions, indeed, a "failure of democracy"? Hardly. The classical concept of democracy, even after the right to vote was extended to women, never included the need for a definite proportion of women among those elected. Neither the idea of equal rights nor the idea of democracy refers to an ideal of actual *mixity* in elected authority—still less to an equal or equitable *sharing* of power. Only the idea of *parity* contains this demand for sharing. It is in this that parity is original and perfectly new, both from the point of view of principles and democratic life itself.

In the case of elective functions, parity can be instituted in two ways: either through organizing, when possible, new ways of voting (of a binomial nature) so as to obtain an *equal number* of elected men and women, or by putting forward an *equal number of candidates*, men and women. The *parity of candidates* seems to me to represent the best solution. It can be easily applied to the list system of voting and to the legislative elections themselves, by taking into account, party by party, the overall number of candidates.

This second method would perhaps be a bit less stringent, and it would give way to internal competition within the parties, but it does have its disadvantages. By being less strictly arithmetical, since the final number of men and women elected would be variable, this method would correspond well with the idea that parity is not simply quantitative but somehow more qualitative. It is the general principle of mixity that counts, more than the exactness of the numbers. We shouldn't quibble over a few seats. In general, there is always something rigid about the purely quantitative, which adapts poorly to human relations.

If *candidacy parity* is so rarely advocated as a method, it is because it runs up against, they say, article 4 of the Constitution, which provides for parties "to organize their activities freely." The argument does not hold, *if* the nation links the objective of parity with democracy (which it can do by way of referendum). In this case, it is not clear how a law concerning candidacy parity undermines the freedom of parties any more than other legal rulings (such as a minimum age to be eligible for candidacy, for example). Party organization does not enjoy a limitless freedom: above all, it must conform to the principles of democracy. Thus there is no real reason not to impose a candidacy parity on the parties. As a general rule, the legal objections have no great merit, this being so much a question of basic political choice. It comes back to the nation to resolve this kind of debate.

It is clear how new the question is, and it would be poorly treated, in one sense or another, if we stuck only to clever legal means. It may be tempting to wish to include parity within equality, in order to water down the idea's originality and make it easier to swallow. But it would be less rigorous and, consequently, more difficult to defend. It is better, then, to accept the democratic invention it is.

Parity really constitutes a political interpretation of sexual difference. This difference ceases to be the pretext for segregation and becomes the justification for *sharing*. Parity posits that the interest in things public and the responsibilities attached devolve to men and women equally. This *sharing* constitutes a realization of sexual difference that does not hierarchize, according to traditional schema, nor neutralize, according to a universalist conception. If it is possible to escape the hierarchical programming of difference, it really would be by inventing original solutions not by denying a priori that this difference takes on political meaning.

However, if many invoke an ideal of actual mixity for political proceedings (even the fiercest adversaries of the institution of parity, indeed of quotas), few ask themselves on what principle this idea of mixity should be founded. No one dares contest this ideal, as if it were self-evident, but they recoil in the face of the questions it raises, because these questions inevitably lead back to the status of sexual difference about which French universalism wants to know nothing.

Even those who wish that political power were *more* shared between men and women are often loath to accept implementing the *means* to arrive at this end, because it seems so shocking to institute mixity through regulations, institutional measures, or—horror of horrors—constitutional changes. Some remain so inconsistent, calling loudly and strongly for "more women" in the Assembly while refusing to take gender difference into account in the civic arena. But if the civic space shouldn't recognize gender, there's no reason to raise the question of the number of men or women in institutions. In reality, those who are so frightened by the means are hardly convinced of the legitimacy of the ends themselves.

This is why, before addressing these new stakes in the relations between the sexes represented today by parity, I returned at length in the preceding pages to the nature, validity, and universality of sexual difference.

If being a woman truly constitutes *one of two essential ways of being a human being*—and only if we agree on this point—then we must admit that a people, no matter what people, also exists according to this double mode. We cannot agree that man (in the generic sense) only exists as divided and deny a nation this double way of being. I agree with Blandine Kriegel's analysis, which bases the legitimacy of sexual equality, according to the model of parity, more on the doctrine of the rights of man than on that of citizenship.[3] It is the equal humanity of men and women that is at stake, more pertinent here than any category of citizenship.

In this sense I would say that the universal mixity of humanity must also find its expression in the definition of the people and must be included in the concept of democracy and the principles of political life.

If we admit this point—which is everything—the debates on the constitutional or legal obstacles become as irrelevant as the constitutionalists' objections to extending voting rights to women once were. Either the cause seems just and the legal consequences must follow, or it doesn't and the fundamental issue must be debated.

Moreover, it is the sovereign people themselves who must judge the soundness of this position and the justice of this cause. According to the Constitution, the people can express themselves by way of Congress or through referendum. Democracy, and this is its strength, has within its means the ability to transform itself: parity, as a *new idea* of democracy, must thus become the object of a decision that is, itself, democratic.*

For all that, I will not spare myself all consideration of the objections raised against the idea of parity and its application, especially since observers often make them in good faith.

---

*Since the first publication of this book in France (1998), the Congress (*Assemblée Nationale* and *Sénat*) was assembled to modify the Constitution. Leaving behind the abstract universalism that had prevented legislation from taking into account the existence of both men and women in political life, the article added to the constitution, voted into law on June 28, 1999, simply stipulates that "the law favorizes equal access of men and women to electoral mandates and electoral functions." Laws have since been passed (in December 1999) requiring political parties to respect parity. Parity has become obligatory for ballot lists. In addition, parties not in compliance with the parity laws risk financial sanctions. *Author's note to the English translation.*

Let us consider then the main objection, which is presented in the following way: Is not the taking into account of the duality of the genders incompatible with the principle of national sovereignty, and thus with the Constitution? It is in these terms that Evelyne Pisier, among others, poses the problem. She declares herself for equality, against parity, supporting her argument with article 3 of the Constitution, according to which a deputy's mandate doesn't come from any one "section of the people."[4] A certain number of arguments recently published in the press have gone in the same direction, holding that parity would place national sovereignty in danger.

Here are two particularly interesting motifs: that of the *indivisibility* of the people, who should not be separated into "sections," and that of national *representation*, through the meaning given to the deputy's mandate. In this case, these two motifs are combined to contest the idea that women can be *represented as such*, since they would thereby constitute a "category" or a "section" of the people. But parity does not only involve legislative elections, and the case of deputies cannot be the only one considered. All the more so because—and many people recognize this—it would be easy enough to apply parity at the level of local elections and whenever the list system of voting is used, as for the election of the European Parliament.[5]

Let us first consider the question of divisibility.

Holding a mandate from no one *section* of the people, the male or female deputy cannot be mandated by a category of citizens. Thus she or he cannot be, so to speak, the elected official of women. That much is certain, and we will come back to it.

Before explaining our idea of parity in representation, let us express a few reservations about the nature of the objections.

The question of knowing *from whom* one holds a mandate is not an issue in the question of parity. This principle is one of a just proportion of women and men among those elected, but it involves no division, no *section* of voters. No one has ever suggested a separate vote for men and for women, nor that each elect their own representatives. Reference to the "section of the people" should not be invoked here, since there is no separate representation of each of the sexes.

The principle, first declared in 1791, according to which it was forbidden for any section of the people to appropriate sovereignty could not have applied to either municipal elections or, especially, to women. Furthermore, it is rather paradoxical today to object to power sharing between the sexes by putting forward a 1791 statement that forbids a monopoly of sovereignty to any one part of the people, when the text itself applied, at the time, to an exclusively male population. Certainly, in this context, women were not in danger of dividing the Republic, since they were not part of it. A posteriori, we cannot help but consider this male population as a "section" of what we think of today as the people. Without interpreting the texts anachronistically, we might emphasize that the absence of women in the eighteenth-century political sphere is not without consequences for readings of texts written in that period, and thus for how these texts may be used today. Because if men are justified, acting among themselves, in prohibiting divisions—which can still be debatable—and if they cannot *then* imagine the duality of the genders, we are no less justified *today* in saying that this duality runs through the electoral body and that it is futile to return to the past to prohibit it. At any rate, the recognition of this duality—and even power sharing between the sexes—would not entail, for all that, an appropriation of the exercise of sovereignty. The exercise of sovereignty shared between the two sexes means, rather, that *neither of the two attributes the exercise of this sovereignty to itself*, contrary to what has taken place up until now.

As for the argument of indivisibility, it has already served quite often in other times to combat the same causes. The logic seems familiar. Indeed, national sovereignty is not the only object of the fantasy of indivisibility and, before dividing the nation, women's claims threatened the unity of another institution that, more than any other, should not allow itself to be shared: the family. It was this argument of indivisibility that was leveled against extending voting rights to women in France at the end of the Second Empire and under the Third Republic. To allow *several* votes in *one single* family was to risk destroying it. For example in 1867, opposing the vote for women, Jules Simon said: "The family has one vote, if it had two it would be divided, it would perish." The motif is always the same: to divide is to substitute plurality for the unity of one thing, to corrupt it, to destroy it. Let us note that the fear of seeing politics divide the conjugal couple is symmetrical to the fear of seeing sexual difference divide the nation. But we know that the family has not perished. What has disappeared is the identification of the entire family with the patriarch and the eclipsing of woman by the masculine identity of the couple. Similarly, what parity threatens is the Republic's identification with a masculine political community, and not the Republic's unity.

The patriarchal family resisted its political division for so long that attempts to tamper a bit with the idea of representation began. Toward the end of the nineteenth century, when it became increasingly difficult to deny women any political existence, and since there was no question of depriving husbands of their power and prerogatives, the idea that women need not vote personally since they were, in fact, represented by their husbands was advanced. This original use of the concept of representation revealed, if it were necessary, that it was masculine power and the *private* subordination of women that were creating obstacles to their freedom and public existence. Society was then ready to grant women their civic rights on the condition that they lose them upon marriage. This clever solution required the unequal treatment of women according to whether or not they had a husband, but the safeguarding of family unity was well worth this slight anomaly, at least in the eyes of the experts: "It seems to us that by constituting the husband as the representative of his voter wife, and in conferring to divorced, single, and widowed women the right to personal suffrage," the law would fulfill the goal of the principle of sovereignty: all women would be represented."[6] It is obvious that "the law" is open to any arrangement provided that wives do not vote. A reading of these old arguments, with the legal acrobatics they proposed, is always instructive: it shows that when a problem is political it should be resolved politically, and thus democratically, and not by appealing to experts.

Even if they do not constitute a simply natural category, since their status may vary, women constitute a historical and cultural category: their exclusion from citizenship *as women*, for a century and a half should have then led to a definition of the conditions of their inclusion. Public affairs had been too much men's affairs to avoid redefining what they could be *with women*. But such an accounting would, precisely, have invited the creation of certain rules, even the consideration of the need for power sharing. In contrast, by becoming "citizens like any others," that is masculine or neuter, women citizens could enter into the Republic *without dividing it*.

To the contrary, the principle of parity consists in having women *as such* enter into decision making, in particular in the National Assembly. But I would like to show that the ideal of mixity of the Assembly, taken as a whole, is not a matter of dividing citizens into categories or communities.

Parity ought to be the mixity of "national representation" *in its entirety* in order to represent the mixity of the nation *in its entirety*. There is not, at least according to my approach, a representation of one group of citizens by a group of elected officials. This sort of division exists, but it is the result of the political role of parties and raises other questions.

We have already seen that this isn't a matter of dividing the body of citizens itself, since no one dreams of separating male and female votes. Some have mistakenly supposed that the mixity of the legislative body, by requiring national representation—and thus the Assembly—to be half men and half women would mean that each of the "halves" would respectively represent the male citizens and the female citizens, thus dividing the nation that must remain one and indivisible.

This is not how parity should be understood. It is not, in any case, the interpretation I would like to give it. To avoid misunderstandings, it is useful to return to the most classical meaning of representation. If parity is foreign to a "communitarian" functioning of democracy, it is because it does not imply that deputies must *"represent" each citizen belonging to his or her own gender*. Such a conception would surely contradict the principles of a representative democracy.

There should be no need to stress that the so-called problem of the "representation of women," that is, their presence and number, only presents itself within the framework of a *representative* democracy since, in a direct democracy where women, hypothetically, would be citizens, they would automatically share sovereignty in proportion to their number. But that is precisely why the political status of women deserves to be questioned in a representative regime where, although they are citizens, women mysteriously disappear from national representation.

It must be that something is happening at the level of the election of representatives that causes women to disappear. As it is not the voters who seem responsible for this magic trick, it is clear that it takes place at the time of candidate registration. This is why, taking into account the cultural and historical reasons barring women from access to candidacy, even the survival of a masculine model of politics, it is desirable to organize parity at the level of candidacies.

The solutions are well known; we have mentioned them: either we can grant equal access to candidacy—in other words, candidacy parity, even if this means imposing parity on the political parties—or we can arrange the parity of elected officials. Parity among elected officials presupposes a new sort of ballot, for example a binominal ballot, as Françoise Gaspard has proposed.[7] In this case, citizens would all decide upon two candidates of their choice, a man and a woman, and, in order not to multiply the number of deputies by two, the number of districts would be divided in two. There would thus be, according to Hubertine's wish, "as many women as men" in the Assembly, or, with the first solution, *approximately* as many. I have explained above why the parity of candidacies might be preferable. But the question remains open.

No matter which method is adopted, once again, this does not imply that the women elected would specially represent female citizens more than male ones; it would mean that women would be equally *present* within the legislative body. Indeed, we must be vigilant on this point. To the extent that deputies "represent" the nation as a whole, and not one part of the electoral body, whatever that one part may be, women *should not be represented separately* (as if, voting separately, they were choosing women representatives). We would be closer to such an idea if we created a women's party appealing for votes for their candidates because they are women. It would thus be a matter of expressing women's common interests (if such an entity existed) within the framework of political pluralism, and no law forbids this. Such a party would claim to represent women *as such*, but this separatist representation would essentially be part of the pluralist functioning of democracy.

It is well known that the hypothetical case of a women's party has nothing to do with the idea of parity. The conflict between the sexes would have to become truly bitter to reach such an extreme, and, in keeping with the parties' call to govern, masculine power and feminine power would have to alternate. . . . To say that political life must allow women their place does not imply that women should form a coherent group standing in solidarity. Sexual division is human and must be recognized in the state. This division must find its political expression, in the larger sense of the term, but it should not be tied to various political choices and interests; these must be left to the judgment of each man and woman. In other words, the politics of the sexes is not entangled in the the usual political divisions, it crosses them, all the while remaining relatively independent—except when the ideology of a party is explicitly antifeminist. This is why women can be in agreement here, independent of political divisions.

I mention the existence of the parties to relativize somewhat the exaggeratedly monolithic view of the National Assembly and the Senate we sometimes wish to take. The simple fact that there are two assemblies, and not just one, which are both elected according to different balloting methods, already shows that national representation can be somewhat modified. Furthermore, not only are the representatives elected quite often as a function of their party membership but also the parties form groups within the assemblies. Representation is less indivisible in practice than in theory. There is thus a bit of feigned naïveté in seeing the duality of gender as the only division capable of threatening "national sovereignty."

Nevertheless, it is not my intention to defend a *more exact* representation of the nation—in fact, quite to the contrary, if that would mean that all categories (social, professional, regional, religious, ethnic) of the population must actually be represented in proportion to their number in the country.

Such a notion would cause the concept of political representation to slip toward the idea of an Assembly exactly reproducing social diversity in its entirety. To explain this slippage, it may be illuminating to make an analogy between these two types of political representation and two types of representation that pertain to the arts. A photographic image is not a constructed representation. A photo (or an *indicating** image) retains a faithful trace of the photographed subject (just as a poll seeks to register the opinions of the moment), while a pictorial or theatrical *representation* (termed *iconic*) somehow invents and constructs a *figure* in order to make what it is "representing" more intelligible and perceptible.[8]

Political *representation,* it seems to me, is a matter of figuration and not copying, because it is not a question of exactly reproducing the thing but, rather, of inventing a *figure* that expresses it and can replace it. This is very similar to the way that Montesquieu conceived of political representation.

---

*The word in French here, *indicielle*, does not translate exactly as "indicative." This adjectival form, derived from the verb *indiquer*, to indicate, lends the notion of the quality of pointing toward something or, in this context, representing it through a sign. Thus the translation "indicating" corresponds to the verbal form "to indicate." *Tr.*

The nation's representatives are mandated by the nation to debate and decide in its place: they are not the mere mouthpieces of the citizens, nor are they the mouthpieces of those in the constituency electing them; just as the assemblies are not the meetings of ambassadors, each delegated by some group or another. The National Assembly, in this respect, need not exactly "reflect" the people who elected it, any more than the deputies need passively repeat, within representative proceedings, the supposed will of the voters, even if democracy, by its nature, asks the nation's representatives to *translate* this will to the best of their ability. The modern conception of politics has a tendency to increasingly forget the principles that underlie the advent of the representative regime in France. According to these principles, the national will *does not exist* until the representatives have themselves expressed it after having debated and decided. It is in this sense that political representation gives form or figure to the national will. The fact that the national will *does not exist* outside the persons and the organs of representation is troubling, and yet obvious: Where then might we find this will? Surely not in the scattering of diverse opinions through which the polls seek to discern an opinion, if not a will. Public opinion is *never* found in the interminable addition of subjective preferences gathered by polls or random interviews. If we walked with a mirror all over France, would we be able to see an image of France in it? Public opinion can only be recognized after the fact, in the discourse gathered and constructed, in the sound sense or analysis formulated by attentive intercessors—no matter who they are. In the same way, political representatives together elaborate what will become the legitimate national will. They thus construct a "representation" of this will that, to be just, must not reflect people's day-to-day opinions but, rather, create a synthesis of the most general and the most legitimate aspirations. (This does not imply that politicians should remain deaf to public opinion or scorn the places where that opinion is expressed. But that is a whole other debate.)

We have not lost sight of the question of the representation of women—quite the contrary.

It is now clear that the equitable *representation* of women in the assemblies does not mean that the women elected must be the mouthpieces of women: this vision of things would be a return to a segmenting by categories. As subtle as the difference between these two ways of conceiving of representation may seem—as reflection or figure—we must maintain them and not confuse the democratic demand for a good "representation" of the social body with what Francine Demichel calls, in rejecting it, "a photography of social diversity."[9]

Parity thus means that the actual mixity of the assemblies must *figure* the human mixity of the nation. The equitable *representation of men and women*—because neither sex should be considered unilaterally—if it is not the faithful *reflection* of the diverse components of the population considered in its empirical reality at a given time, should thus be a *relevant figure* of what the people are, universally, that is, a people made up of men and women. Through their *presence* in the Assembly, men and women "embody" the nation for the period of their mandate.

Certainly, the representatives sent by the people to "express will" in their place are also each chosen for what they are and for what they propose to do, by which voters more or less recognize themselves. But the Assembly in its totality and multiplicity, which is going to debate and decide, must be, more generally, a sort of *imitation* of the people, in Aristotle's sense of the term. The image, a product of imitation, is not a servile copy but a *fiction*, an image composed to better show what it represents and that, because it better reveals it, is more true than the reality of which it retains only the principle traits.

This figurative dimension of representation retains the trace of the origin of political representation as it appeared in Hobbes. The sovereign monarch *represents* the people as an actor, or a character represents the author of a play on the stage. We are still far from representative regimes, but, as the true author of power, the people are recognized as the source of political authority in the final analysis.

This theatrical vision of representation will, alas, leave other traces: notably the idea that the sovereign, and later, sovereignty, are indivisible and should be indivisible. Because, if the people (this disturbing multitude) must be figured, it is to substitute *one* for the *multiple* and put an indivisible body—that is, an individual—in the place of the multitude. At first, power could only "represent" the people if it was embodied in one single person. Thus, for Hobbes all are subject to the monarch, while for Rousseau each person joins with all others, and the general will—a new political fiction—will come to avert the risks of the division of the people.

The problem of democracy will always be reconciling the need for unifying representation with the preservation of a political life that allows, both publicly and politically, for the expression of contradictions, divergences, and differences.

To reconcile these two needs, political and human plurality must be represented, that is to say present, within the assemblies themselves. And political divisions, through the existence of the parties, and the human duality of the sexes, through parity, must not be obscured.

Today it is up to us to extricate ourselves, if possible, from a fear of division that democratic life should help combat, since democracy rests precisely on the political resolution of conflicts and not on authoritarian unification or consensual harmony. The greatest dangers in politics do not necessarily come from that which divides but often from the violence of forced unification.

What is disturbing in parity, however, as in the recognition of universal sexual difference, is precisely its power of *division*. Parity collides with the desire for a unifying political representation, still marked by what we previously called the *nostalgia for the one*, as well as the fear of division: a metaphysical fear and also a political fear. A fear of divided man, a fear of democratic conflict.

These fears do not only touch power itself or its theoreticians, they touch the masses who are also afraid of their own divisions. They are often ready to sacrifice their freedoms at the altar of unity, as La Boéthie taught us, or nearer to our time, Claude Lefort.

However, as Nicole Loraux demonstrates by returning to the Greek origins of the city-state,[10] division is not only a formidable threat of dissolution, that rupture that can destroy or dissolve the city-state, it is also, like sedition (*stasis*), like conflict, that which shakes up the state and prevents it from becoming fixed in a stultifying calm. To this extent, division is a factor in a certain kind of cohesion. We can thus speak of a "bond of division," of a division *that unites* as much as it separates.

The state is not a unity but a *plurality (plêthos)*, Aristotle repeated (him again!), in opposition to Plato of course and, by anticipation, in opposition to all those who succumb to the anguish of division in political matters.

If politics—including the politics of the sexes—consists in resolving conflicts together rather than quashing them, division should be claimed as a value: the value of difference versus uniformity, of conflict versus immobility.

It is up to the two sexes to accept their differences, to defend the value of the mixed, of the heterogeneous. And to say that the progress of democracy toward parity would constitute a just break with the forced, masculine unification of the political community.

Tomorrow, the mixity of the assemblies could represent the dual face of the people, just as man and woman are the two faces of the human.

⊓⊙TES

CLARİFİCATİ⊙⊓S: PREFACE T⊙ THE E⊓GLİSH-LA⊓GUAGE EDİTİ⊙⊓

1. *Making Sex: Body and Gender from the Greeks to Freud* (Cambridge: Harvard University Press, 1990) (*La fabrique du sexe, essai sur le corps et le genre en Occident* [Paris: Gallimard, 1992]).

2. de Beauvoir, *Le deuxième sexe* (Paris: Gallimard, 1978), p. 13.

3. These testimonies are drawn from the work of E. Dubreuil, unfortunately titled *Des parents du même sexe* (Paris: Odile Jacob, 1998), pp. 141 and 159.

4. Sometimes, myths and theories add other natural or divine conditions. "For the Baruya, children are the product of the sexual union of a man and a woman and the intervention of the Sun." See Maurice Godelier and Michel Panoff, *Le production du corps* (Paris: Editions des archives contemporaines, 1998), p. 3.

5. Françoise Hériter, *Masculin/Féminin, La pensé de la difference* (Paris: Odile Jacob, 1996), p. 230.

6. Augustine, *The City of God*, 14, XI.

7. Marcela Iacub, "Reproduction et division juridique des sexes," *Les Temps Moderne* 609 (2000).

8. Ibid.
9. In 1984, Benoîte Groult was president of the commission for the feminization of names of occupations, created by Yvette Roudy.
10. Maurice Grevisse, *Le bon usage*, 12th ed. (Paris: Duculot, 1991), p. 795.
11. Ibid., p. 791.
12. "Adresse à Monsieur le Président de la République, protecteur de l'Académie française," *Le Figaro*, 9 January 1998.
13. Marc Fumaroli, "La querelle de neutre," *Le Monde*, 31 July 1998. Italics are my own.

PREFACE

1. Notably Simone Veil, Gisèle Halimi, but also Monique Pelletier, Yvette Roudy, Véronique Neiertz . . . and many others.
2. In keeping with the the French usage of the words *sexe* and *sexué*, which signify both an ineffaceable and given condition of human existence (also proper to most living beings, a category to which we belong) and an interpreted and socialized form of this essential condition. Sex is not an essentially biological reality but an anthropological, global, animal, historical, and political reality—inseparably. *Author's note to the English translation.*

MAN DIVIDED

1. *Le Propre du langage* (Paris: Editions du Seuil, 1997), p. 37.
2. I am referring here to the discourse of transsexuals, not to the possible psychoanalytic interpretation of transsexuality.
3. See Catherine Millot, "Gabriel ou le sexe des anges," in *Horsexe: Essai sur le transsexualisme* (Paris: Galilée, 1997), p. 19.
4. Contrary to what Jean Baudrillard appears to believe. See *Ecran total* (Paris: Galilée, 1997), p. 19.
5. Colette, *The Pure and the Impure*, trans. Herma Briffault (London: Penguin, 1971), p. 86; Colette, *Le Pur et l'impur* (Paris: Le Livre de Poche, 1992), p. 112.

6. Françoise Héritier, *Masculin/Féminin: La Pensée de la différence* (Paris: Odile Jacob, 1996).

7. Charles Blanc, *Grammaire des Arts du dessin, architecture, sculpture, peinture, jardins, gravure* (Paris, 1876), p. 21.

8. Arlette Farge, "De la différence des sexes," in *Des Lieux pour l'histoire* (Paris: Editions du Seuil, 1997), p. 133.

9. Jacques Lacan, *Le Séminaire*, book 2 (Paris: Editions du Seuil, 1978) 303, emphasis mine.

10. In *Three Contributions to the Theory of Sex* Freud distinguishes between the sexual "object," "the person from whom the sexual attraction emanates," and the sexual "aim," "the aim toward which the instinct strives" (553). In his essay on sexual aberrations, he argues that in certain cases, such as voyeurism and exhibitionism, the sexual aim might take on an "active" and/or a "passive" form (569). In his discussion of sadism and masochism, Freud indicates a distinction between active and passive sexual "attitudes" (570). For Freud, of course, passivity and activity are generally associated with femininity and masculinity respectively. See Sigmund Freud, *Three Contributions to the Theory of Sex* in *The Basic Writings of Sigmund Freud* (New York: Random House, 1938). [*Tr.*: I have translated the expression "*pulsion à but passif*" quite literally since the author takes up the question of the activity or passivity of the "aim" immediately hereafter.]

11. Alain Etchegoyen sets off again in search of this natural difference in his beautiful *Eloge de la féminité* (Paris: Arléa, 1997). Unfortunately, he allows himself to be guided a little too much in this quest by Jean-Jacques Rousseau.

12. Single-celled beings that reproduce through division and not sexually are not mortal (at least in principle).

VERSIONS OF DIFFERENCE

1. André Masson, *Le Rebelle du surréalisme: Ecrits* (Paris: Hermann, 1976), p. 135.

2. *La Politique du mâle* (The Politics of the Male) is the French title of

the American Kate Millett's book published by Stock in 1971. The original title was *Sexual Politics* (New York: Doubleday, 1969). It was essentially about denouncing patriarchal domination, which explains my choice of the French translation.

3. *The Subjection of Women* (1869) is translated by Marie-Françoise Cachin as "the subservience (*asservissement*)" of women" (Paris: Petite Bibliothèque Payot, 1975), but it is the idea of subjection, it seems to me, that is important here.

4. I explored this Aristotelian theory of generation in "Le tout premier écart," in *Les Fins de l'homme* (Colloque de Cérisy, Paris: Galilée, 1981).

5. Aristotle, *Politique* 1.5.1252b.

6. *L'Odysée* 9.114. [*Tr.*: I have translated the French translation of the Greek. The English translation of the Greek is as follows: "Each one rules his wives and children as he pleases." See Homer, *The Odyssey* 9.138–139, trans. William Cullen Bryant (Boston: Houghton, Mifflin, 1871), pp. 180–181.]

7. *Politique* 1.5.1253a.

8. Ibid. 1.1.1252a.

9. Ibid. 1.13.1259b.

10. Aristotle, *Histoire des animaux* (Paris: Les Belles Lettres, 1968); *De la Génération des animaux* (Paris: Les Belles Lettres, 1961).

11. Aeschylus, *Les Euménides*, 658–661, cited by Jean-Pierre Vernant in *Mythe et pensée chez les Grecs* (Paris: François Maspero, 1980), 1:133. [*Tr.*: Again, I have translated from the French translation of the Greek to maintain continuity in the author's argument. The English translation (one among many of course) reads: "The mother to the child that men call hers is no true life-begetter, but a nurse of live seed. 'Tis the sower of the seed alone begetteth." See Aeschylus, *The Eumenides*, trans. Gilbert Murray (New York: Oxford University Press, 1925), p. 33.]

12. Vernant, *Mythe et pensée chez les Grecs*.

13. Jacques Lacan, *Ecrits* (Paris: Editions du Seuil, 1966), p. 692; Jacques Lacan, *Ecrits: A Selection*, trans. Alan Sheridan (London: Tavistock, 1977), p. 287 (translation modified).

14. Freud's article is from 1925. It is translated into French in *La Vie sexuelle* (Paris: PUF, 1973), p. 123 ff.

15. Beginning in 1926, Karen Horney contests the infantile ignorance of the vagina, poses the question of the social valorization of the penis, and hypothesizes the masculine repression of a desire for maternity. See *La Psychologie de la femme* (New York, W. W. Norton, 1967 and Paris: Payot, 1969).

16. Simone de Beauvoir, *Le Deuxième sexe* (Paris: Gallimard, 1978). The first edition appeared in 1949; Simone de Beauvoir, *The Second Sex*, trans. H. M. Parshley (New York: Vintage, 1989), p. 45 (translation modified).

17. Antoinette Fouque, "Il y a 2 sexes," *Le Débat* (Paris: Gallimard, 1995), p. 175.

18. See Nicole Loraux, *Les Enfants d'Athena* (Paris: François Maspero, 1981), p. 66 and *Points Essais* (Paris: Editions du Seuil, 1990.) See also *Né de la terre: Mythe et politique à Athènes* (Paris: Editions du Seuil, 1996).

19. Hubert Damisch, *Un Souvenir d'enfance par Piero della Francesca* (Paris: Editions du Seuil, 1997).

20. This is why the most fruitful research on the difference between the sexes has begun with the philosophical "deconstruction" of the "metaphysics of presence"—for example, the work of Jacques Derrida, most notably from *De la grammatologie* (Paris: Editions du Seuil, 1967), and *L'Ecriture et la différence* (Paris: Editions du Seuil, 1967) to *Glas* (Paris: Galilée, 1974).

FREEDOM AND FECUNDITY

1. I use this expression—"difference of women"—as one would speak of the "difference of painting" in the eighteenth century to designate the specificity of the art of color in relation to drawing or sculpture. See Roger de Piles, *Cours de peinture par principes* (1709, Paris: Gallimard, 1989).

2. de Beauvoir, *Le Deuxième sexe*, vol., part 2.

3. Ibid., 1:455; *The Second Sex*, p. 385.

4. See on this subject Cather Chalier's beautiful book, prefaced by Emmanuel Lévinas, *Les Matriarches* (Paris: Editions du Cerf, 1985).

5. de Beauvoir, *Le Deuxième sexe*, 1:34; *The Second Sex*, p. xxxiv.

6. *Le Deuxième sexe*, p. 81; *The Second Sex*, p. 62.

7. *Le Deuxième sexe*, pp. 82–83; *The Second Sex*, p. 63.

8. In an earlier work, I addressed this question of the other via the motif of the event. See *Critique de l'égocentrisme: L'Evénement de l'autre* (Paris: Galilée, 1996).

9. *The Second Sex*, p. 63.

10. *Le Deuxième sexe*, 1:285; *The Second Sex*, p. 267.

11. *Le Deuxième sexe*, 2:157–158. *The Second Sex*, p. 496. [*Tr.*: I have altered the English translation to correspond more closely to the original text as well as the author's rendering of it.]

12. Angelus Silesius is a seventeenth-century mystical poet. He writes in *Le Pélerin chérubinique*: "La rose est sans pourquoi, fleurit parce qu'elle fleurit. N'a souci d'elle-même, ne désire être vue." (The rose is without why; it flowers because it flowers. It cares not for itself; it desires not to be seen.) Heidegger comments on these lines in chapter 5 of *Le Principe de raison* (Paris: Gallimard, 1962). *The Book of Angelus Silesius: With Observations by the Ancient Zen Masters*, trans. Frederick Franck (New York: Knopf, 1976); Martin Heidegger, *The Principle of Reason*, trans. Reginald Lilly (Bloomington: Indiana University Press, 1991).

13. "La mère a l'illusion pacifiante de se sentir un être en soi, une valeur toute faite." *Le Deuxième sexe*, 2:157–58. (The mother enjoys the comforting illusion of feeling that she is a human being *in herself*, a value.) *The Second Sex*, p. 496.

THE MASCULINE UNIVERSAL

1. Susan Moller Okin, "Sur la question des différences," in *La Place des femmes: Les Enjeux de l'identité et de l'égalité au regard des sciences sociales* (Paris: La Découverte, 1995), p. 63.

2. The International Congress for the Rights of Women (Congrès international du droit des femmes), July 29–August 9, 1878. See Maïté Albistur and Daniel Armogathe, *Histoire du féminisme français* (Paris: Editions Des Femmes, 1977), p. 350ff.

3. The Congress of Civil Rights and Women's Suffrage (Congrès du droit civil et du suffrage des femmes), June 1908. See Albistur and Armogathe, *Histoire du féminisme français*, and Mme Zylberberg-Hoquart, *Féminisme et syndicalisme en France avant 1914* (third cycle thesis, University of Tours, 1973).

4. de Beauvoir, *Le Deuxième sexe*, 2:55. This translation is my own.

5. Author of *La Femme et le Socialisme* (1879).

6. This is the case with Elisabeth Badinter's books. In her works, however, the neutralization of difference takes on an original form through the emphasis on bisexual traits in both sexes. See most notably *XY: De l'identité masculine* (Paris: Odile Jacob, 1992); *Xy: On Masculine Identity*, trans. Lydia Davis (New York: Columbia University Press, 1995).

7. Such as the Radicalesbians or the Gay Liberation Front women.

8. "La Pensée straight," *Questions féministes* 7 (February 1980).

IDENTITY AND HOMOSEXUALITY

1. "La famille," in *Claude Lévi-Strauss*, texts collected by Raymond Bellour and Catherine Clément (Paris: Gallimard, 1979), p. 105.

2. Aristotle, *The Politics*, trans. T. A. Sinclair (London: Penguin, 1992) 1.2.1252a (translation modified); *Politique* 1.2.1252a.

3. Catherine Millot, *Gide, Genet, Mishima: Intelligence de la perversion* (Paris: Gallimard, 1987), p. 15.

4. Sigmund Freud, *The Ego and the Id*, trans. Joan Riviere (London: Hogarth Press, 1947), p. 43 (translation modified); "Le Moi et le Äa," in *Essais de psychanalyse* (Paris: Petite Bibliothèque Payot, 1963), p. 202.

5. Interview given to *Libération*, September 3, 1997.

6. Michel Foucault, *Dits et Ecrits*, vol. 4 (Paris: Gallimard, 1994), p. 164.

7. K. J. Dover, *Greek Homosexuality* (London: Duckworth, 1978); J.

Dover, *Homosexualité grecque* (Grenoble: La Pensée sauvage, 1982).
Foucault wrote an article on this text in *Libération*, June 1, 1982. See
Dits et Ecrits, 4:315.

THE DOUBLE ORIGIN

1. *Le Débat* 36, 1985. "Les Droits de l'homme face aux progrès de la
   médecine, de la biologie et de la biochimie" (The Rights of Man in
   the Face of Progress in Medicine, Biology, and Biochemistry).
2. Reference to article 2 of the European Convention on Protections
   (*Convention européenne de sauvegarde*).
3. Françoise Héritier, *Masculin/Féminin,*, pp. 277 ff.

ARISTOTLE OVER/AGAINST PLATO

1. *The Politics* 1.2.1252b (translation modified); *Politics* 1.5.1252b.
2. Plato, *Great Dialogues of Plato*, trans. W. H. D. Rouse (New York:
   New American Library, 1984), book 5. *La République*5.
3. Emmanuel Lévinas, *Totality and Infinity: An Essay on Exteriority*,
   trans. Alphonso Lingis (The Hague: Martinus Nijhoff, 1979); Emmanuel Lévinas, *Totalité et infini: Essai sur l'extériorité* (La Haye:
   Martinus Nijhoff, 1961).

WAR OR POLITICS

1. Karl von Clausewitz, *On War* (New York: Random House, 1943), p.
   16; Clausewitz, *De la Guerre*, trans. D. Naville (Paris: Editions de Mi-
   nuit, 1955).
2. Michel Foucault, *Il faut défendre la société*, course at the Collège de
   France, 1976 (Paris: Editions du Seuil/Gallimard, 1997).
3. Véronique Nohoum-Grappe, "Guerre et différence des sexes," in *De
   la Violence et des femmes*, ed. Cécile Dauphin and Arlette Farge
   (Paris: Albin Michel, 1997), p. 172.
4. See the bibliography, limited but precious, given by Christine
   Dauphin in the notes of her article, "Fragiles et puissantes, les

femmes dans la société du XIXe siècle," in Dauphin and Farge, ed., *De la Violence et des femmes*, pp. 88–103.

ARCHAÏC AND LİBERTİNE FRANCE

1. Claire Duchen, "Féminisme français et féminismes anglo-américains: Spécificité et débats actuels," in Okin, *La Place des femmes*, p. 355. Claire Duchen takes up certain questions posed by Lisa Appignanesi in S. Dunant, *The War of the Words: The Political Correctness Debate* (London: Virago, 1994). [*Tr.*: The author uses the English "date rape."]

2. Mona Ozouf, *Les Mots des femmes: Essai sur la singularité française, l'esprit de la cité* (Paris: Fayard, 1995), p. 11.

3. Ibid., p. 383.

4. Ibid.

5. Elisabeth Guigou, *Etre femme en politique* (Paris: Plon, 1997), p. 102.

6. See the account of Ségolène Royal, *La Vérité d'une femme* (Paris: Stock, 1996).

7. American women have been voting since 1914 (but in the state of Wyoming since 1869!), German women since 1919, English women since 1928. . . .

8. This proportion has markedly increased since the 1997 legislative elections.

9. The Manifesto of the Ten appeared in *L'Express* of June 6, 1996.

10. The charter was adopted May 18, 1996, on the occasion of the European summit: "Women for the transformation of politics and society."

EQUALİTY

1. "That all men are created equal is neither self-evident nor demonstrable." Hannah Arendt, "Vérité et politique," in *La Crise de la culture* (Paris: Gallimard, 1972), p. 314.

2. Expression borrowed from the Latin poet Terrence.

3. On this subject, see most notably Genviève Fraisse, *La Différence des sexes* (Paris: PUF, 1996).

4. See Monique David-Mesnard, ed., *L'Exercice du savoir et la différence de sexes* (Paris: L'Harmattan, 1991).

5. Read about the extraordinary misadventure of this quota in the book by Gisèle Halimi, *La Nouvelle cause des femmes* (Paris: Editions du Seuil, 1997), pp. 107ff.

PARİTY

1. Hubertine Auclert, *Le Vote des femmes* (Paris: Giard, 1908), pp. 136–137.

2. Under certain conditions, women could be represented in the Estates General under the Ancien Régime.

3. See Blandine Kriegel, "Parité et principe d'égalité."

4. Evelyne Pisier, "Egalité ou parité?," in Okin, *La Place des femmes*, pp. 514–517. Article 3 stipulates: "National sovereignty belongs to the people who exercise it through its representatives and by means of referendum. No section of the people nor any individual may attribute to himself this exercise."

5. We owe it to Michel Rocard to have applied parity to the socialist lists for the 1994 European elections, thereby increasing the number of women in the European Parliament.

6. Maurice Renaudot, *Le Féminisme et les droits publics des femmes* (Paris: Niort, 1902), p. 147. Cited in the excellent book by Françoise Gaspard, Claude Servan-Schreiber, and Anne le Gall, *Au pouvoir, citoyennes! Liberté, Egalité, Parité* (Paris: Editions du Seuil, 1992), p. 101.

7. Gaspard, Servan-Schreiber, and le Gall, *Au pouvoir citoyennes!*, p. 173.

8. On this distinction between a trace and a figure, see Jean-Marie Schaffer, "Empreinte biographique et esthétique de la Darstellung," in *La Présentation*, ed. René Passeron (Paris: Editions du CNRS, 1985). See also Régis Debray, *L'Etat séducteur* (Paris: Gallimard, 1993),

p. 31ff. However, while it may indicate, a photo is something other than a "reproduction."

9. Francine Demichel, "A Parts égales: Contribution au débat sur la parité," in *Receuil Dalloz Sirey*, vol. 12, 1996.

10. Nicole Loraux, *La Cité divisée* (Paris: Payot, 1997). I am referring here to chapter 4, "Le Lien de la division."

ÍΠDEX

nomic, 143–44; of opportunity, 146–48; political nature of, 139, 141; positive discrimination and, 146–49; sexual identity and, 142, 143; truth and, 139–40; universality and, 63–64

equity, 129

ethics, 101–5

ethnicity, 14–15

European Convention on the Rights of Man, 102

existentialism, 46–48, 57

facts, 10

family, 99–100; abolishment of, 114, 116, 117–18; indivisibility and, 161; as political association, 26–28, 113; representation and, 161–62; sexual division of labor, 71–72

Farge, Arlette, 9

fecundity, 84–85, 114; abasement of feminine, 42–43; alienation and, 42–43, 53–55; biological destiny, 42–43, 50, 53–54, 58; instrumentality and, 44–45; legal order and, 45–46; meaning and, 48–50; power and, 44–45, 60; rejection of, 41–43, 59–60; sexual identity and, 81–82; subject and, 43, 47–48, 55–57; temporality and, 51–52; women's control of, 48–49; see also maternity

feminism, xxix, 64–68; appropria-

tion of masculine models, 64–66, 74, 76; radical feminism, 76–77; sexism in, 66–67

feminist congress, 68

filiation, xiv–xv, 45, 102–9, 114; genetic origins and, 105–6; as institutional, 107–8

finitude, 50–51

Foucault, Michel, 94–98, 123

Fouque, Antoinette, 37

France, 131–32; Constitution, 155–56, 158n, 158–59; electoral amendment (1982), 151; language, xxiv–xxvii; National Assembly, 136, 154, 157, 158n, 162–68; political life, 135–37; private life, 132–35; Republic, 161; Senate, 154, 158n, 165

freedom, 59, 134; existentialist analysis of, 46–47; foundation and, 56–57; love and, 55–56; nature and, 41–46, 128; as negativity, 47, 50–51

free will, 47

Freud, Sigmund, 4, 10–11, 174(n10); homosexuality, view of, 87–89; political dimension of, 34–35; theory of sexual difference, xix, 30–34

Gaspard, Françoise, 164

Gay Pride, 95

Gay Science, The (Nietzsche), 45, 51

responsibility, 59, 102–4

rights: of child, 102, 104–7; civic rights, 144–45; responsibility and, 102–4

rights of man, 101–4, 140, 157

right to give life, 101–4

Rousseau, Jean-Jacques, 16

sadomasochism, 97, 126, 174(n10)

Sand, George, 134

Sartre, Jean-Paul, 46–47, 50

Second Sex, The (Beauvoir), xxxii, 41–43, 45–48, 52–60, 69–70

seduction, 132–34

self-sufficiency, 83

Senate (France), 154, 158n, 165

separatism, 76–77; parity and, 164–65

"Several Psychic Consequences of the Anatomical Differences of the Sexes" (Freud), 32

sexism, in feminism, 66–67

sexual difference, xxx, xxxii–xxxiii, 99, 173(n2); division of species, 3–5, 12; equality and, 143–44; excluded third, 3, 6, 15, 64–66; French view, 133–35; Greek view, 111–19; hierarchy of, 8–9, 14, 25–29, 38, 113; irrelevance of, 62; nature and, 6–8; parity and, 156–59; politicization of, 23, 78; rejection of, 41–43, 59–60, 64–65, 111–12, 114–16; social constructions, 16, 127–28; transsexualism,

5–6; transvestism, 6–7; *see also* sexual identity; versions of difference

sexual identity, 3–4, 41, 84, 99; equality and, 142, 143; fecundity and, 81–82; Freudian view, 87–89; love and, 84–87; marriage and, 81–83; *see also* homosexuality; sexual difference

sexuality, 59; biological *vs.* social, 84; heterosexual relations as oppressive, 76–77; as independent of reproduction, 86–87; *see also* homosexuality

Simon, Jules, 161

single person, 91

social constructions, 16, 127–28

social sciences, 9–10, 150

souls, 5, 86, 117

sovereignty, 160–61, 169, 181(n4)

Spinoza, Baruch, 51

subject, 150; fecundity and, 43, 47–48, 55–57; homosexuality and, 87–88; as neuter, 13, 33–34, 62–65, 65, 77, 129, 150

subordination of women, 25–28

subversions, 5

surrogate mothers, 105

temporality, 51–52

thought, 50

tolerance, 90–91

traditional societies, 81–83

transcendence, 47, 52–53

European Perspectives
A Series in Social Thought and Cultural Criticism
Lawrence D. Kritzman, Editor